As I Was Saying ... Observations on International Business and Trade Policy, Exports, Education, and the Future

As I Was Saying ... Observations on International Business and Trade Policy, Exports, Education, and the Future

Volume 1

Michael R. Czinkota

Illustrations by David Clark

CETERUM CENSEO

businessexpert
Press

As I Was Saying … Observations on International Business and Trade Policy, Exports, Education, and the Future. Volume 1.
Copyright © Business Expert Press, LLC, 2012.

First published in 2012 by
Business Expert Press, LLC
222 East 46th Street, New York, NY 10017
www.businessexpertpress.com

ISBN-13: 978-160649-411-0 (paperback)

ISBN-13: 978-160649-412-7 (e-book)

DOI 10.4128/9781606494127

Collection ISSN: 1948-2752 (print)
Collection ISSN: 1948-2760 (electronic)

Cover design by Jonathan Pennell and David Clark
Interior design by Exeter Premedia Services Private Ltd., Chennai, India

First edition: 2012

10 9 8 7 6 5 4 3 2 1

Printed in the United States of America.

To Ilona, who helps me more than I can say

Contents

On Thinking Ahead **89**

Foreword

For more than thirty years, Professor Czinkota of Georgetown University has been a contributor of editorial commentary on the international business field. His work has been published in outlets ranging from the *Asian Wall Street Journal* to the *New York Times*, *Roll Call* to the *Washington Times*, *Financial Times* to the *Handelsblatt*, and *The Japan Times* to the *Shanghai Daily*. This work is a reflection of his belief, that all too often business executives and policy makers will not read a lengthy academic treatise or an entire book—but they will consider looking through a short piece of commentary. Czinkota therefore has undertaken to reach out to the market with short writings that reflect his much longer academic journal articles in order to disseminate knowledge and bring about change.

Czinkota's approach is characterized by his addressing of real problems, not concocted ones. Second, he uses a professor's ability to serve as honest broker, using the facts surrounding issues rather than surmised ideas. Third, since he does not believe that medicine has to taste bad in order to work, he injects a dose of humor in his contemplations. He explains what linkages exist in an interactive world and he does so with a focus on captivating the understanding and interest of the reader. He takes some pretty boring-sounding issues of global import, and translates them into our daily lives. In doing so he also addresses unconventional issues, for example, how the charges of the ladies of the night in Eastern Europe reflect the travails of emerging economies; why it is better for all of us to pursue new auto jobs rather than import quotas; how a devalued dollar affects international sellers and buyers alike.

Czinkota is prone to provide a strong encouragement of open trade relations. However, he does not just see or present policy, business, or research issues from one side only. His extensive experience in the business field, policy positions, and in academic research allows him to seamlessly glide between these three worlds, understand and analyze the different perspectives, and show, how these have been re-calibrated over time.

The fact that he was born in Germany and raised in Scotland, Spain, and the United States is clearly demonstrated in his comparative comments, which allow the reader to better understand the varying prism of perspective by other nations. His international work experience in five continents makes his commentary reflective of cultural constraints and varying expectations. He captures these dimensions both in word, and then, for each commentary, also in cartoon. With the artistic support by David Clark—an award-winning and syndicated cartoonist—he ensures that the reader can quickly take the voyage between sight and word, and even hard core analysts will not be able to avoid cracking the occasional smile.

Enjoy this book which provides short, delectable morsels of reading.

Philip Kotler
The S.C. Johnson & Son Distinguished Professor
of International Marketing
Kellogg School of Management
Northwestern University,
Chicago
January 8, 2012

Introduction

Why You Should Read This Book

In my many commentaries and editorials over the decades, I provide a long-term perspective of issues, campaigns, and phenomena. Going beyond the flavor of the month and conveying a perspective of historic embeddedness is the key purpose of this book. We can learn from the past, not only by understanding what was done before us, but also by appreciating the context in which changes occur. The commentary format allows the reader to escape the major studying approach. Ongoing involvement with policy makers and firms has taught me that many people do not read academic books or even high-quality journal articles. Working one's way through them is typically considered too laborious and insufficiently stimulating. However, decision makers do read short pieces, articles, and commentaries. The opportunity to communicate with leaders is much higher with the short piece. Of course, the comments usually need to be based on a background of significant research and understanding of an issue. Yet, short writings are instrumental in bringing issues to the fore, and, eventually, in precipitating understanding and perhaps even change.

Over the decades, international business and trade have mushroomed in importance. Social and economic shifts have taken us from the back room discussions of experts to public disputes around the world. From ignorance we have entered the stage of too much information. A new sense of transparency and accountability offers new directions to businesses and their executives. The emergence of a public moral sense and scrutiny about injustices in connection with many things international encourages companies and governments to reduce corruption and abandon unsavory practices.

The role of governments has changed drastically, first shrinking in the 1980s and 1990s, but now coming back with a vengeance, dictating the direction and strength of international business activities. After decades of aiming for more open markets, even the liberal trading nations and the trade supporting politicians within them, are developing a tendency to restrict imports and encourage exports. In blatant disregard that someone's export has to be someone else's import, governments try to keep home industries protected and their own economies stable and revitalized. Yet, in spite of many efforts to that effect, global imbalances are persistent and distortive.

Viewed over the long haul, however, we can distinguish patterns of ebb and flow in the international business and trade arena. Today we often find the claim that "if it's not on Google it does not exist." However, long-term observers recognize that , just like Saint Augustin who prayed in about 400 A.D. "Lord, make me chaste, but not yet" policy makers and executives often develop strong if not nontransparent measures to delay or even defeat the easing of international trade and investment flows. There are also the times where change cannot happen quickly enough, where everyone aims to streamline and fast track legislation and international accords by limiting the influence of deliberate legislative votes.

There are the subtle and not so subtle efforts at sanctions and disruptions of trade flows, yet they are often met by opposing interest levels, which, due to historical developments, tend to negate such restrictions. Repeatedly we see one side, which is losing contracts, blaming it all on the corruption and nepotism on part of the winners. Yet, culturally, the closeness to family and desire to help one's own environment in a home country context, may be seen as an obligation rather than a deviation. Laws can be seen as rigorous structural supports for economic development, or as substantial barriers to growth.

The use and meaning of terminology also has its (often temporary) major effects. For example, for decades, the use of the term "Most Favored Nation (MFN)" status has led to demonstrations and even street battles. Now, the problem has gone away, since governments have changed the terminology and only speak of "Normal Trade Relations (NTR)," a goal that seems to be acceptable to all. Definitions which shape our understanding of core issues such as "fairness," "market gaps," "dumping," and "natural," can be changed or amended, and thus present us with new realities. Nowadays, one discusses and often re-evaluates the meaning and adjustment of key business pillars such as risk, competition, profit, and ownership, which perhaps gradually prepares us for a new environment. Many of today's business executives discover that their activities are but one integral component of society. Politics, security, and religion are only some of the other dimensions that historically, and maybe again in the future, are held in possibly higher esteem than economics and business by society at large. Those who argue based on business principles alone may increasingly find themselves on the losing side.

Futurity in general is, in many ways, not all that innovative, but reflective of ongoing change. Just consider how different things will be in a mere 50 years—keeping in mind that the ballpoint pen only came to the U.S. market in 1945, the computer game Pong only entered the market in 1972, and electronic or email on personal computers only advanced in the late 1980s. Will we look as retro to our descendants as our ancestors appear to us today (if we bother to look)? Yet, at the same time we are only a brief constant in a world of change.

We complain about the new phenomenon of pirates in Somalia—though such profession was riding high in the Caribbean or during Roman times in Sicily (which is where Pompeius earned his early reputation when he brought about their demise). We highlight the disruptions from terrorism but neglect that already the crusaders wrote home about their fear of terror. We debate new approaches to teaching and communication, but don't stop to think what effect Gutenberg's printing press, wireless telegraphy, or the introduction of radio had on business and society. We deplore the differentiation of groups based on religion, but conveniently forget the impact of Torquemada and the inquisition, or the reactions to Luther's theses on the church doors of Wittenberg.

Each article and the accompanying cartoon (remember, a picture can be worth a thousand words) are thought opportunity to chew on, with the reading taking only a very short time—and the major investment being made in the chewing. I hope that the opportunity for comparisons, the recognition of the presence both of rapid shifts but also of permanence, and the appreciation that in many instances the future was 2000 years ago, provides for good thought stimuli. Be it for bedtime reading, for beefing up on a topic before a "wise table dinner," or just for racking the brain, I wish you well with these pages. There is the old Native American saying that "When storms come about, little birds seek to shelter, while eagles soar." By reading and enjoying this book, you are hopefully likely to prefer the altitude of the eagles!

I am grateful to my wife Ilona Czinkota who gives me the time and is willing to read and comment on my writings. Thank you to my daughter Margarete who is a great sounding board for new ideas, and does not hesitate to let me know when something meets with her displeasure. Typically, she is right in suggesting that something is "so last century." Best of all, mother and daughter can come up with excellent suggestions. I also thank the members of my research team, in particular Ireene Leoncio, Elizabeth Garbitelli, and Mariele Marki. Finally, I also thank the editors who let me use the columns that I have written for their newspapers for their kind permission.

On Trade Policy

Time for A North American Trade Policy

When the leaders of Mexico, Canada and the United States meet for a summit in Mexico this weekend, the agenda will include a largely predictable list of topics ranging from the presidency of Honduras to the swine flu. The historic significance of the meeting, however, will flow from what is said, or not said, about the still-undefined U.S. trade policy.

Mexican President Felipe Calderon will protest the U.S. administration's failure to honor its North American Free Trade Agreement commitment (now 14 years overdue) and permit Mexican trucks to

Originally published in *Roll Call*, August 7, 2009. Used with permission of Michael R. Czinkota and *Roll Call*.

operate on U.S. highways. At the same time, Canadian Prime Minister Stephen Harper is likely to press the President Barack Obama on "Buy America" provisions in the U.S. stimulus package that discriminate against non-U.S. suppliers and violate a host of U.S. international commitments—from the Word Trade Organization to NAFTA.

But the crucial issue will be whether there will be a new vision and consensus for a North American trade policy. The past decades have seen many bilateral agreements. Increasingly, however, the problems to be addressed and solved are larger than the individual capabilities of such bilateral agreements. If there is to be success in solving major problems, then there needs to be close collaboration between the three nations in recognition and acceptance of their interdependence.

In conjunction with their legislatures, each of the three governments has drawn up important plans. The goals range from improved competitiveness to energy independence, leadership in green technologies, migration control and health care reform. All of these issues require close cooperation between the North American partners.

The talks in Mexico must become a teachable moment on the subject of trade policy and, specifically, how trade liberalization and open markets are key to building a new kind of competitiveness. In the past, any definition of competitiveness depended on whether the perspective taken was that of the government, the firm or the individual. Typically, the government was mainly concerned about tax revenue, companies were worried about profitability and individuals were focused on keeping their jobs. Today's definition of competitiveness newly includes and reflects one's neighbors. Even though such transborder perspective may be difficult for Congress—and for legislators in Mexico and Canada—there needs to be a recognition that it is geographic proximity that affects housing prices, trust and perceptions of risk and prosperity. If several houses in a neighborhood go up for public auction, prices of all other houses suffer. Collaboration creates jobs, promotes energy independence and environmental sustainability, and makes use of the economic power of the world's largest regional market. Proximity matters.

Obama, Calderon and Harper have a unique approach to articulate a new vision of global competitiveness based on a North American platform. Major elements should include:

- A credible commitment to reject protectionist measures. One step in this direction would be a solution to unjustified restrictions against the Mexican trucking industry and to "Buy America" issues. Congress needs to overcome parochialism and accept 'local' politics that are inclusive of our neighbors. Given the complementary nature of the three countries—in terms of human, capital and technological resources—we need new ways to deepen economic integration, not to raise barriers.
- Recognition of the critical role that energy plays in our collective competitiveness through an action plan which eliminates distribution inefficiencies and creates a more effective integration of the North American energy grid.
- A plan for a single North American effort for clean energy development, a common approach to carbon offsets and the use of energy leadership as a key joint competitive tool.
- An insistence on joint leadership in the creation and enforcement of global standards for corporate veracity, public accountability and decisions regarding what's for sale and what shouldn't be.
- A Congressional acknowledgement that migration flows and economic success are linked. Doing so will redefine return on investment calculations for economic development spending. It will also broaden the Congressional perspective when tradeoffs between international economic liberalization and national security are considered.
- Options for health care treatment for patients on a North American basis. Here Congress can find new options that maintain quality of care standards while giving proper

consideration to variations in cost structure within the region. While one does not want to see the emergence of unregulated and unrestricted regional medical tourism, it is important to make use of existing regional health technology assets and capabilities.

Economic and trade concerns have grown in size. We need a cluster of collaboration that enables us to find solutions which are reflective of North American needs, accepted by the local culture and affordable with regional resources. Congress and the administration should consider a tie-in with our North American neighbors to broaden the horizon of possible improvements in our society.

Doomsayers Are Wrong: Don't Count Out U.S. Economy

Worldwide commentary would make it appear as if the United States has become a global economic burden. The current decline of the dollar leads to dire predictions of sharply reduced military strength and shrinking political influence. These commentators are sadly mistaken.

For them, endurance typically refers to the upcoming weekend. Such forecasters need to consider for the United States what other nations have long asserted for themselves—a perspective framed by the long term.

Originally published in *The Washington Times*, January 14, 2008. Used with permission of Michael R. Czinkota and *The Washington Times*.

For example, in a recent discussion of global economics, a Chinese acquaintance readily agreed that his nation had perhaps had a bad century - but he asserted that China was now ready to again become the center of the world. In discussing Turkey's desire to become part of the European Union, an Austrian friend repeatedly recalled the Ottoman Empire's attack against Vienna—in 1683.

Leading powers always suffer from voices of discontent. But other than key players in the past, U.S. encouragement of free speech leads to global discussion rather than underground communication. Think of how the United States was attacked globally in word and action in 1917, in 1941 and many times since then. Though President Reagan was greatly mourned on his passing, when he held office, cartoons showed him as a cowboy drawing his gun. Only rarely would there be a picture showing the positive impact of U.S. strength and determination on the architecture of the global economy.

Over the past 60 years, the United States has consistently been the key contributor to world economic growth and welfare. In the 1940s, its leadership created the World Bank, the International Monetary Fund and the General Agreement on Tariffs and Trade—now the World Trade Organization. These three pillars reduce global poverty, support financial flows and set fair rules for all participants in international trade. In the 1970s, U.S. courage and conviction led the move from gold-related fixed exchange rates to floating ones. This shift allowed the money supply to grow and gave rise to world economic abundance.

The United States has continued to set an example for the world of how market-based actions consistently produce very efficient and effective results. For decades, the country has been the economic locomotive, absorbing growing foreign production within a large and wealthy domestic market. Of course there have been missteps—as one would expect to encounter with any pioneering efforts—but the U.S. approach has worked better than any others when it comes to economic improvement.

Economic stability has been a hallmark for the United States. Consider the effect of political discord or the transfer of power on an international level. Sadly, such events are all too often accompanied by descriptions such as "smoke was rising over villages and cities." In the United States - even though sometimes there appears to be a tearing of hair shirts and the threat of emigration—political transitions and changes come about smoothly, without bloody battles or economic destruction.

U.S. society tends to admire the "winners" of economic competition and appreciates the accumulation of wealth. Government, in turn, typically does not try to take away from achievers. There is, of course, the government tax bite, but you pretty much get to keep what you've accumulated. That sounds like a minor issue until one observes that in many countries over the course of several generations such experiences are quite unusual.

These are the factors which set the United States apart from other nations and affect the investment behavior of the world. For decades, experts predicted the crash of the dollar. Now, the "chickens coming home to roost" arguments predict major economic decline. Some forecasters have even breathed a sigh of relief that their dismal future has finally been sighted.

There is no reason to lose heart due to temporary setbacks. The United States continues to present new and special opportunities to the world. It offers the security and safety that have sadly been unattainable for most people on earth. It presents a vision, flexibility and capability to adjust to new conditions which are envied around the globe.

Let us use a long-term perspective to appreciate past effects and future prospects. Global investors are not foolish when they show their reluctance to turn away from the dollar. What determines the value of money in the long term is the trust, the promise and the future that a nation offers to those holding its currency. To the forecasters full of dismay, I suggest: Don't write the United States off too soon—remember that the Roman Empire lasted more than 700 years—the Ottoman Empire almost 600. Yes, sometimes it is lonesome at the top.

Currency Flow and Trade: Implications of the Port Debate

The policy eclat over the acquisition of selected U.S. port operations by Dubai appears to be over. There were threats by Congress to pass legislation prohibiting such ownership, countered by statements that President Bush would veto any such legislation. Now, the Dubai owners have decided to spin off the U.S. operations from the global conglomerate which they have purchased. Yet, there may be significant long-term consequences for currency values and trade practices.

Originally published in *The Washington Times*, March 26, 2006. Used with permission of Michael R. Czinkota and *The Washington Times*.

Most of the public discussion of this sordid affair has reflected the growing sensitivity in the United States to ownership and control of assets by non-domestic entities. The debate has focused heavily on possible discrimination against Muslim investors, protection against terrorism in U.S. ports and retaliation against U.S. investors abroad.

What appears to be not yet widely understood are the potential effects that these and similar policy decisions (such as the Unocal walk-away by China) can have on the value of global currencies and on trade flows. Congress' law of unintended consequences may strike again: The short-term direct effects of this action are likely to be far outweighed by the long-run indirect effects.

The United States has experienced more than 20 years of current-account deficits. It imports more than it exports. In past years, every month has brought more news about growing trade deficits, now up to $68.5 billion per month. It is hard to remember that President Nixon decided to abandon the fixed-exchange rate system for the Western world because of an annual imbalance of $5 billion. But we do see in more recent times that, typically, nations with a current-account deficit above 5 percent of gross domestic product (GDP) have experienced grave domestic and international consequences.

Even though the current imbalance is approaching 6 percent of GDP, these harsh consequences have not occurred in the United States. The conditions are special: They are influenced by a high willingness of other countries to hold U.S. dollars, a substantial ability of foreign individuals and institutions to lend those dollars to the United States and a high U.S. capability to embed the dollar as a global currency. As a result, there is a surface picture of tranquility which has abounded in global trade and currency markets.

However, we know that this trend will have to change. Eventually, the United States will have to export more and import less. The key questions are how to achieve such change, how long to wait for such change and whether it should occur through market forces or through government intervention. It does appear that in addition to growing international competitiveness of U.S. firms, changes in the value of the U.S. dollar are needed to reverse the astounding trade imbalances.

The Dubai withdrawal may well be the watershed that triggers shifts in exchange rates now. The congressional debate, the national posture and the global repercussions may well form the basis of new Plaza Agreement-type conditions, which will gradually drive down the value of the dollar for the long term.

The pronouncements by Congress, the growing public debate and the withdrawal plans of the foreign investors directly play to the emotions of investors. The message is clear: Investments and ownership by foreign capital holders will be scrutinized with new rules, and may well be attacked, rejected or publicly scorned. This will be done regardless of plans made by the administration or commitments made to global agreements.

In other words, confidence in the U.S. dollar has been challenged by the U.S. itself. We know that money is just a piece of paper. What matters most in setting its value is the psychology behind it—the trust, outlook and confidence in the government that has issued the money. Investors may be shaken by the public response to the port-acquisition plans, but Mr. Bush's steadfast embrace of foreign funds is an important counterpoint which reduces the urgency of the concerns, lets any shift come slowly and results in a soft landing.

The uncertainty and therefore the risk for anyone holding dollars or dollar-based assets has now increased. Such a change influences the perceptions of investors and their actions. Fewer investments from abroad into the United States and a decrease in dollar holdings will depreciate the price of the dollar, making imports more expensive and exports cheaper. In addition, continued discussions may affect U.S. public opinion and eventually change the views, brand preferences and country-of-origin sensitivity of American buyers.

This almost kabuki-like political interaction on port ownership may well presage a long-delayed and necessary shift in trade outcomes. What appears to be an unfulfilled policy debate on foreign investment may yet stimulate important changes in trade patterns which are based on market forces rather than government intervention.

Economic Stimulus Plan Must Incorporate International Trade

President-elect Obama is defining his economic stimulus plan. Nations around the world attempt to stabilize their economies as well. Typically, each nation's emphasis rests with domestic issues. Though politically understandable (GM is more important to the U.S. than Toyota), a successful plan must reflect the powerful influence of international trade on the national economy. In the U.S., for example, trade related activities comprise more than 25 percent of its economic activities—which is more than the housing and banking sectors combined. Trade also accounted

With M. Smith. Originally published in the *Korea Times*, January 19, 2009. Used with permission of Michael R. Czinkota and the *Korea Times*.

for the entire U.S. economic growth in the past year. Trade issues definitely qualify for top priority, but seem to be neglected so far.

The world depends on continuity in trade. The global economic outlook, competition and consumer choice are shaped by trade flows and currency values. Competitive devaluations, for example, provide unfair advantages to exporters. For many nations, the promotion of exports must have a central place in their economic recovery package.

In the U.S., the national debate about economic recovery includes many lessons from the Great Depression. The clearest of these is to avoid the protectionism of the Smoot Hawley tariffs that turned a market crash in the U.S. into a global Great Depression.

Global leaders give lip service to this conventional wisdom but there is a gap between co-mmuniqué language and on-the-ground practices. Indonesia and Russia have already begun to raise their protection of domestic industries—to the detriment of global trade. The Doha Round of international trade negotiations continues to be stalled—even though eight years of negotiations have placed great benefits within reach.

The U.S. experiences some difficulties in its global position, but around the world there is hope, expectation and willingness for a re-emergence of U.S. leadership. There is growing concern among U.S. trading partners that the new Congress and Administration might introduce a new era of U.S. protectionism. Global markets are parsing any announcement for signs of what the Obama Administration will mean for them.

The world economies are intertwined. Any stimulus measure of one nation is likely to rapidly affect others and trigger responses. Economic activity is highly concentrated among a few players. The United States, European Union, Japan, China, and Canada account for more than 75 percent of the world's economy. A good domestic stimulus should not become an international distortion. Subsidies paid to farmers in one country, for example, can affect dairy related industries around the world. Once introduced, protectionism can quickly become contagious and be emulated around the world.

The economic recovery plan is both an opportunity to send a signal to markets about what they can expect in terms of U.S. trade, and a chance to provide the benefits of U.S. leadership on the global stage. Discussions of U.S. economic improvements must include a focus on global recovery. Countries must be able and willing to buy each other's goods—in an increasing quantity—if world economies are to blossom.

Here are some recommendations:

- Countries need to make unambiguous, consistent, and clear statements that industry bailout packages will not include protectionist measures. In the U.S., the newly appointed performance czar should assess economic stimulus measures by the U.S. and its trading partners for any inappropriate subsidies of exports or discrimination against imports.
- We need a renewed commitment to the World Trade Organization and its stalled Doha Round of trade negotiations. Rules need to be consistent and strong. The key players in world trade need to re-energize the negotiations by making major commitments and taking "early harvest" of potential agreements on a plurilateral basis. One first step could be the elimination of tariffs on environmental goods and services.
- The U.S. must lead its economic partners on the basis of trust and fair play, applied to trade and investment rules as well as to currency values. We're in this together. The sound implementation of policy objectives—be they health care, education, retirement—require a sound economy which depends on global collaboration on trade.

Trade success can provide the momentum which keeps economies from stalling out before the stimulus can kick in. Trade issues must move up to the front burner.

New Auto Jobs, Not Quotas

U.S. automakers are in dire straits. While non-U.S. brands are gaining market share, both GM and Ford have announced major plant closings and substantial layoffs. For some, these announcements have raised the specter of a return to the policies of the 1980s, when the United States imposed "voluntary" export restraints on Japanese importers. But new conditions faced by today's producers, consumers, markets and politicians should prevent us from re-using tools that were not even successful a generation ago.

Originally published in *The Japan Times*, February 4, 2006. Used with permission of Michael R. Czinkota and *The Japan Times*.

The two remaining traditional U.S. automakers—General Motors and Ford—are both experiencing major losses in their U.S. operations. The reasons are manifold, ranging from restrictive union contracts and high health-care costs to poor model choices and rapid market shifts. The upshot is a dramatic shrinking of these companies, both as employers and as market players.

Ford has announced plans to close up to 14 plants and eliminate up to 30,000 jobs. GM also plans to reduce its workforce by 30,000 and shutter 12 plants.

In 1985 the Big Three U.S. automakers owned three-quarters of their home market; today GM and Ford hang on to less than one-third of domestic sales. Some of those sales have only been accomplished because of major international input into product design.

At the same time, U.S. investments by foreign car companies are thriving. The Japan Automobile Association reports that its members have opened 28 plants in the U.S. with more than 55,000 employees. Honda, Nissan and Toyota manufacturing abounds in Ohio, Alabama, Michigan and Mississippi. If one were to add the employment created in their dealerships, these firms account for more than 415,000 U.S. jobs.

The Korean firms Hyundai and Kia are following in their footsteps. They are investing heavily in facilities in California and Alabama. This means that automotive industry jobs remain, but they are created by firms not native to the country.

Consumers are much less concerned about whether a brand is domestic or foreign; they worry about quality and price. Increasingly the issue of fuel consumption comes up. In times of skyrocketing gas prices, they don't want to be saddled with paying more for protecting manufacturers of U.S. origin. They often perceive nondomestic brands as having a higher reputation.

Long gone are the days when employer parking lots required owners of foreign cars to park outside. Newspaper classifieds no longer separate listings of foreign and domestic cars. And rightfully so—who can tell the difference?

By comparison, public procurement has remained behind the times. For example, in spite of high quality and performance, we see very few police departments purchasing Volvo products, even though Ford acquired the Swedes in the last millennium. There seems to be lingering concern by local officials about a voter backlash.

The same worries some policymakers at the national level. There is the desire to lead in a new direction, to reverse a company's decline and to help constituents. Many workers and their families have suffered through job losses. We need to remember that even if jobs are exchanged at a macro-level between firms in an industry this does not mean that laid-off workers in Detroit will be the ones hired in Canton, Mississippi.

The competitive platform is new. Toyota and other foreign producers are battling each other; they see fellow importers and investors as the competition. They worry about what is yet to come from abroad. For example, what about future imports of the Logan from France's Renault, which has a sticker price of $6,400?

They plan for the onslaught of cars developed in, say, Malaysia, China or Vietnam? They listen very carefully when the founder of a car company in the past announces plans to regale the U.S. market with the Chery from China.

Key issues concern quality, fuel efficiency, service, safety and low prices as well as research, development and innovation. How will the European Union react to growing automotive import pressures? How can Chinese brand manufacturers such as Geely be convinced to invest rather than import? One can even build an argument linking production expertise with national security.

The U.S. is very fortunate that the market share shifts has not resulted in a replay of the textile industry's migration abroad. Its large market size has attracted a slew of foreign direct investments and will continue to do so. These investments reflect the continued competitiveness of the U.S. production infrastructure, the capability of local economies to adjust and the flexibility of the workforce and suppliers.

Maintaining these advantages and helping displaced workers find new opportunities are of crucial policy concern. The location of a car company's headquarters should not be.

LAW of UNINTENDED CONSEQUENCES

Free Trade Carries a Hefty Price

U.S. President George W. Bush's decision to impose tariffs on steel imports into the United States has been decried as a politically motivated and economically ruinous move that marks the end of free trade and initiates a battle in the World Trade Organization.

We could, of course, dispatch our experts again to WTO hearings and start the traditional international charges and countercharges. The better alternative is to use this occasion to informally delineate a U.S. trade strategy that lets our industry and foreign friends know where we stand and where we are headed. Doing so will provide predictability to

Originally published in *The Japan Times*, March 18, 2002. Used with permission of Michael R. Czinkota and *The Japan Times*.

the market and consistency to our decision-making, both of which will increase market confidence.

Here are the components of our trade strategy: First is world leadership. The U.S. carries the leadership mantle due to astute policymaking, a willingness to contribute to the greater global good, and fortuitous developments in history. Some of our allies desire to be the leaders when it comes to international economic standards but are happy to let us bear the burden of armed conflict or the risk of terrorism. Global leadership is not a partitionable function, applicable to only a few issues: It is all encompassing.

Next are the benefits of leadership. We don't know how long the currently unassailable position of the U.S. will last, but world history tells us that positions can change. Past leadership is good for prominence in the history books, or for minor privileges, such as Greece's position of first flag carrier during the Olympics. Past accomplishments do little when it comes to resources or influence. Just think, in 1948 the U.S. almost launched the International Trade Organization, which would have streamlined global commerce. We didn't push hard then and the effort failed. It took almost 50 years to relaunch such an institution—now called the World Trade Organization, which still does not have the same strengths as the ITO would have had. It is important to make hay while the sun shines. Britain, long in decline, was able to draw on the resources acquired during the height of empire for more than half a century. The U.S. will get things done now and also acquire bankable resources for a rainy day.

Third, we need ongoing international help in counting our blessings when it comes to free trade. Every elected official has many vocal constituents recount vivid tales of travails caused by imports. The positive effects caused by free trade are not self-evident; they must be explained, defined and provided by industry and our trading partners on a regular basis, particularly when it comes to jobs. As far as congressional votes go, trade-related employment effects are the currency of the realm.

Fourth, in a global world, local issues are important. When it comes to trade, expectations of a perfect track record may be the enemy of good achievements. Trade is only one component of the mosaic of mankind's activity. Policy needs to reflect the broad scope of human desires and needs. The steel decision needs to be seen in such a context. There is a political price tag associated with strong U.S. support of free trade. The rare and limited protection of a domestic industry with much leverage is such a price.

During the anthrax scare, the U.S. government negotiated rather harshly with Bayer, the producer of Cipro. Some claimed that such an approach was in violation of long-standing support for intellectual property rights. Realistically, it is an emergency-appropriate deviation from the established routine, a necessary price of past and future enforcement consistency.

Fifth, our trade strategy is balanced. The fact that jobs matter also helps the free traders. As the chairman of the congressional House Small Business Committee stated: "I will watch very carefully how the steel tariffs affect the steel users and exporters in my district. And if jobs get lost, I will pounce!" Our representatives have become familiar with global concerns. In the future, international trade actions will perhaps mainly be addressed domestically, after a battle between, say, sugar vs. steel interests.

Was the steel decision political? Of course it was, in the sense of exercising the art of compromise. The decision also defines new boundaries. It has a clear context, provides direction and promises containment. It demonstrates U.S. leadership and, simultaneously, strengthens the world trade framework.

U.S. Needs to Revamp Trade Policy

This election's promise of a fresh mandate for the next administration provides an opportunity for writing a new chapter in U.S. trade relations. Just as our foreign policy now addresses a new world order, our trade policy must do the same. While it may be politically expedient and provide narcissistic gratification to continue bashing Japan's trade practices, it is not going to produce the desired results.

Much more productive will be the reorientation of trade policy, making it more domestic. Such an approach will reduce the pressure on government to pry open foreign markets through politics and instead will

With M. Kotabe. Originally published in *The Dallas Morning News*, December 13, 1992. Used with permission of Michael R. Czinkota and *The Dallas Morning News*.

concentrate on providing firms with the strategic skills and environment to be competitive. Even if the private sector knows that a lighthouse is needed, it still can be hard and perhaps impossible to build one based on private initiative alone. There must be a government-business partnership that pools resources and skills and enables us to compete globally.

We propose four areas for immediate policy-maker attention:

Information: Despite the widespread existence of information, its accessibility and subsequent use are comparatively weak in the United States. Government action tends to concentrate on bailing out failing industries rather than providing an early warning system alerting business to the potential for failure. Information highways need to track and evaluate competitive developments worldwide and make the information available to U.S. industry.

Collaboration: Government should actively encourage collaboration among companies, particularly in areas of rapid technological change, substantial social need and intense international competition. That collaboration should focus both on product and process technologies in fields such as environmental safety, healthcare, materials development and other leading-edge technologies. At the same time, common concerns, such as quality performance, should be addressed in cooperative efforts industrywide and include both suppliers and customers.

Export promotion: The U.S. economy still exports less than it could. Many firms do not participate in the international market because they must act rationally, according to domestic economic realities. For example, the short-term start-up cost and the higher transaction cost can make it uneconomical for a firm to go international when investors demand quarterly performance gains. While it will be important to work on changing the short-term orientation of capital markets through fiscal policies that enhance the capacity of U.S. firms to invest, there is also a dire need to overcome the short-term gap by providing export assistance to firms.

Human capital: There is a clear need to find, develop and disseminate the best educational resources this country has to offer. Using educational talent locally is a luxury America can no longer afford. Technology now allows our best educators to be available nationally. Electronic instruction and video systems, offering national access to the best teaching methods and contents, must be regular parts of primary, secondary and trade education within and outside of corporations. Just as agricultural universities and railroads advanced us in the 1800s, high-technology education can become the switch to the right track of the next century.

U.S. economic performance has its shortfalls. Some are a function of our domestic economic behavior, others the result of changing global realities. The bottom line is that we cannot afford to continue an exclusive reliance on rugged individualism. The nation must pursue opportunities for collaborative action between industry and government, focused on broad national gaps in the fields of research, technology and information. That is the trade policy of tomorrow, designed to make U.S. products and performance so desirable that others abroad simply can't afford not to deal with U.S. firms.

Dollar Devaluation: Cure for Trade Deficit?

With a projected 1985 trade deficit of over $140 billion, the U.S. is desperately seeking a cure for its chronic trade imbalances. In search of causes for the deficit, various suggestions have been paraded in front of us.

At first, Japan was blamed because of its use of market targeting practices and its market access restrictions. After much public debate, it was concluded that these practices only accounted for a portion of the trade deficit. After all, our deficits with other countries were rising as well.

Now the high value of the dollar has become the major culprit. While we are not certain about the extent to which our high dollar value causes

Originally published in *The Japan Times*, January 25, 1986. Used with permission of Michael R. Czinkota and *The Japan Times*.

our deficit (the estimates range from 50 to 90 percent), legistlators, business leaders and labor seem to agree that the major cause of our poor export performance is the overvalued dollar.

As a result, the solution to our trade deficit becomes clear. A reduction in the dollar's value would make our products less expensive and more competitive abroad. Dollar devaluation therefore appears to be a clear cut, relatively painless, measureable, and effective remedy.

However, before engaging in a single-minded drive to devalue the dollar, let's think about the desirability of such action and its potential repercussions.

First, a decrease in the value of the dollar may reduce the amount of foreign investment flows into the United States. Such a loss could have serious consequences. Our budget deficit is being financed by foreign money, and even if stringent budget tightening measures are adopted, the deficit will still be substantial for a number of years. Since our domestic savings rate is too low to finance these deficits, we need to attract foreign funds. If we lose those funds, the public sector debt will crowd out our own private sector credit demands, leading to higher interest rates.

Second, the devaluation of the dollar would raise the cost of imports. A portion of the price increase would be absorbed by foreign manufacturers, and we would see some decline in imports. The vast majority of our $370 billion import bill, however, would increase in price. Adding to that the indirect effects of higher import prices, namely an increase in prices charged by import competing domestic industries, indicates that a dollar devaluation would result in a commensurate price increase for at least 10 percent of our GNP. This would precipitate a dramatic domestic inflationary push.

Third, when engaging in any concerted action to drive down the value of the dollar, the question invariably arises how far is far enough? Once the dollar begins to decline precipitously, dollar withdrawals by foreign individuals and financial institutions will follow rapidly. Although the United States is still considered a good country to "park" one's money in, because of high interest rates and economic stability, these benefits evaporate quickly when a foreign treasurer sees his capital shrinking with the decline in the currency's value.

Since private sector financial flows outnumber governmental flows by about 10 to one, we could be stimulating an avalanche of dollar flights over which we would have no control.

There is a final major rationale for cautioning against blaming only the dollar for our trade performance. The current focus on the dollar value conveniently places the onus for change on foreign shoulders and macro variables. Such finger pointing threatens to make our exporting firms complacent. Businesses may be under the false impression that they are doing well, and that they only need to wait for the dollar to drop to become competitive again.

So, is there any sound advice to give? We need to realize that it is a good sign if foreign countries and individuals are willing to invest in the United States. Domestic demand for such foreign investment should be reduced, but without scaring off foreign investors. A balance must be found between discouraging and encouraging financial flows into the United States, since, as usual in life, too much of a good thing can be dangerous to our health.

Furthermore, we need to recognize that there is a limit to the usefulness of exchange rate measures. Their side-effects can easily threaten the domestic economy and their impact is limited if foreign governments devalue their currencies competitively. Also, financial market intervention by governments can only serve to strengthen or weaken the free market flow of capital, but will not reverse it. Therefore, we need to vigorously attack and change underlying factors that precipitate the investment flows, such as our demand for funds (financing U.S. consumption and the budget deficit) and our high level of real interest rates.

We need to strengthen our efforts to remove obstacles and barriers to market access abroad, and to reduce unfair foreign trade practices. In today's economic climate every country tries to increase exports and limit imports, and the danger is very real indeed that more and more unfair trade practices will emerge. We need to stem this development through international negotiations, and strong arm tactics if necessary, since the very existence of the world trade framework is at stake.

Finally, we need to concentrate on restoring the international competitiveness of our domestic industry. Neither dollar devaluation, nor any governmental action will provide the wonder drug necessary to reduce the trade deficit permanently. It is ultimately the responsibility of individual businesses to regain and retain their market positions.

Since the days of pure price competitiveness are over, improvements must come about through productivity increases, marketing, service and quality innovations, and the development of unique international competence in current and future market niches. Unless the private sector takes the lead in harnessing all its resources to develop a strategic national market advantage, all public sector efforts and discussions will be for naught.

U.S.-Japanese Trade Strategies

Now that the public outcry over U.S.-Japanese trade relations has quieted down temporarily, it is worthwhile to take a calm and detached look at the bilateral relationship and consider reorienting our approach to solving trade problems between our nations.

The focus of the United States on the size of the bilateral deficit as a measure of Japanese good faith in market opening has made the threat of trade retaliation against Japan, Washington's most predictable annual international trade event. Thus protectionist "rite of spring" is touched

With P. Kollmer. Originally published in *The Japan Times*, May 13, 1985. Used with permission of Michael R. Czinkota and *The Japan Times*.

off by the discovery that the bilateral trade deficit has become worse than ever. U.S. trade negotiators rush to correct the imbalance by demanding specific policy changes from the Japanese in various industrial sectors.

Congress, provoked by parochial concerns, then throws a more or less collective tantrum that increases the stakes of the negotiations. Sensitive to menacing signals from Capitol Hill, Japan finally announces "major" policy and regulator changes. U.S. policy-makers then belittle these policy modifications as too shallow but accept them as signs of goodwill and the crisis is quelled. That is, at least, until the next year when it is discovered that the bilateral trade deficit has worsened, and the cycle of mutual hostilities is reinitiated.

The belief that the U.S.-Japanese bilateral trade deficit is synonymous with Japanese protectionism leads to hasty and shortsighted reactions on both sides of the Pacific. We hunt for negotiation trophies that have only a shortlived impact, while the Japanese offer "extorted" policy changes, which show no results in terms of the trade deficit. Obviously, the spiral of accusations and excuses will not solve trade problems in the long run.

Indeed, every year the exchange becomes more and more acerbic, and, as the deficit figures move from an unacceptable to an intolerable level, an avalanche of protectionism will eventually be precipitated, possibly followed by irreparable political alienation between the two nations. A long-term strategic vision of U.S. international trade posture must become the basis of U.S. trade policy and drive our negotiations with Japan. This long-term view should be two-tiered: We should seek to reduce protectionism worldwide and to increase U.S. exports. The belief that a reduction in Japanese import barriers will automatically translate into a substantially reduced U.S. bilateral deficit over-simplifies the dynamics of trade among competing nations. It also leads to a willingness to sacrifice the benefits of international trade on the altar of the next election.

The U.S. trade deficit did not accumulate overnight and poor U.S. exports are not the product of one afternoon of Japanese mercantilism. America's inadequate trade performance has become universalized. The Japanese contribution to the overall U.S. trade deficit, for example, has actually declined from 57 percent in 1981 to 33 percent in 1984.

Years of a strong dollar and a history of ill-equipped U.S. corporate overseas marketing efforts have made a substantive contribution to the trade deficit that can hardly be obviated by several days of Congressional browbeating or by narrowly focused periodic negotiation efforts.

Indeed, the importance of these other factors to the buildup of the U.S. trade deficit implies that U.S. trade negotiation strategy with Japan should aim beyond the bilateral deficit and focus on reducing the size of the global Japanese trade surplus.

Time-phased targets need to be set for a reduction of Japan's overall surplus. This can either be achieved through increased penetration of the Japanese market by importers or through a global protectionistic backlash against the Japanese.

This focus on Japan's overall trade surplus has several benefits. First, it would result in a greater ease of future negotiations, since it would place the burden of eliminating protectionist barriers where it belongs: squarely in the lap of the Japanese.

U.S. negotiators would no longer be forced to nitpick over regulations perceived as inhibitive to U.S. exports. The Japanese would have to assume the responsibility of identifying and dismantling barriers to imports and not content themselves with begrudging acquiescence to U.S. demands for specific policy changes.

Shifting the burden to the Japanese makes sense. After all, no one knows which policies, regulations or attitudes discriminate against imports in Japan better than the Japanese do.

Second, this approach would compel Japan to extend its market opening efforts beyond consumer goods, which constitute only a very small portion of Japanese imports.

Industrial goods, commodities, services, and investment and monetary policies would have to be included in the liberalization activities.

Third, Japan would be forced to realize that the ultimate test of market opening efforts is not regulatory reforms, but resounding ringing cash registers of importers.

A focus on the surplus would take into account Japan's dependence on trade and its desire to expand its trade activities, yet balance these objectives by limiting the pain that can be inflicted on the economies of other countries.

The threat of global restrictions on its exports would provide Japan with substantial incentive and impetus for rapid domestic policy action.

Such an approach might represent an unprecedented management of international trade; it would however, ensure real market-opening results rather than a shifting of market share among countries.

Finally, this approach would add a multilateral emphasis to a long-run strategic focus on U.S.-Japanese realignment.

The FCC and Trade Barriers

Mark S. Fowler, chairman of the Federal Communications Commission (FCC) has announced that the commission is considering steps to restrict access to U.S. markets by imposing strict technical certification procedures on Japanese manufactured telecommunications equipment.

Offhand, it might seem like a good idea to use the commission as another tool in developing a trade policy stance toward Japan. Given our 1984 trade deficit of $123 billion, with $33 billion of that accounted for by Japan, it appears that we should pull all registers to reduce the deficits.

Originally published in the *Chicago Tribune*, April 28, 1985. Used with permission of Michael R. Czinkota and the *Chicago Tribune*.

Because the telecommunications trade imbalance between the U.S. and Japan alone was about $2 billion last year, this industrial sector just might be a good one to start with.

But there are several issues to consider in following such an approach. Is an industry-specific retaliatory policy viable? An industry-specific focus permits us to address narrowly defined, specific problems, and perhaps resolve them quickly. We can tailor retaliatory action to focus only on the telecommunications industry, leaving other activities unaffected.

But this approach completely disregards the stated goal of increasing trade. Our trade policy should not harm the U.S. firm using foreign telecommunications components or the U.S. consumer buying them, nor should we keep our domestic producers free from foreign competition. What we rightfully ask for is increased market access for competitive U.S. telecommunications, their domestic markets and other foreign markets. The retaliatory approach not only totally negates the recognition of comparative advantage and further deteriorates the flow of trade, but it makes the initial objective of market access even more difficult to attain.

A second, even larger issue emanating from the FCC considerations is that of the locus of control of trade policy. By involving regulatory agencies, we run the very real danger that U.S. commercial policy will be determined by a new and growing chorus of discordant voices. This is particularly the case since regulatory agencies see themselves mainly responsible to Congress or to specific constituencies rather than to the administration. We also need to keep in mind that FCC regulatory action designed to exert trade retaliation does not narrowly focus on our bilateral relations with Japan.

Telecommunications is a multilateral issue since virtually every country has a regulated communications system which restricts the market access of imports. Involving the FCC in international trade policy is a poor idea. It would jeopardize the delicate fiber of free trade developments which we have begun to weave domestically through our negotiations for free trade zones and our attempts to create a more cohesive and unified trade policy stance, and which we strive for internationally with our calls for a new round of trade negotiations. FCC involvement would increase rather than reduce the role of big government and would give impetus to building up nontariff barriers rather than tearing them down.

Should We Regulate Services Trade?

In the past few months the United States has reached agreement with its allies on tigher controls on computer exports, including for the first time controls on software trade, and has proposed regulating exports of certain services to the security forces of countries that aid or abet international terrorism.

The international trade community should pay close attention to these two events, for although they seem to be unrelated and to address quite narrowly defined issues, they mark the beginning of a new era: we are beginning to regulate the export of services.

Originally published in the *Journal of Commerce*, August 7, 1984. Used with permission of Michael R. Czinkota and the *Journal of Commerce*.

It may seem far-fetched to search for major implications in these minor regulations and proposals. Experience teaches us, however, that most major regulatory efforts begin with relatively small and non-controversial steps.

One could react to these initial efforts with outrage at yet another type of ill-advised government regulation, but such a reaction would lack perspective. In the past decade, as the United States has become an increasingly services-based economy, exports of services have grown in importance, representing an area in which the United States has a substantial comparative advantage internationally.

As long as the United States is willing to regulate the exports of products in order to enhance its national security or foreign policy objectives, it seems only reasonable to develop regulations for services, especially when one considers that many services have potential military usefulness.

At the same time, however, U.S. officials charged with developing a policy for regulating trade in services need to think of the consequences of such controls. Just as the country was able to build a lead in products trade in the late 1940s and 1950s that resulted in strong international economic and political ties for 30 years, it now has a chance to build strong and lasting services linkages with countries around the world.

In order to be successful in this process, however, we need to realize that, unlike the 1950s, the 1980s are a time of great competition in international trade, and many other countries are rapidly increasing their service capabilities. If we hesitate too long or regulate too much, we may miss a unique opportunity to resume an eminent leadership position in world trade.

It is imperative, therefore, that the United States move into the area of services regulation with its eyes open. We should not develop regulations in an ad hoc, haphazard, indirect, or fragmented fashion and then apply them to entire industries by analogy.

We need to develop a regulatory policy that is well defined, enforceable, and tolerable to U.S. industries and allies. Such an approach can serve U.S. national security and foreign policy goals without endangering our economic competitiveness abroad.

Trade Sanctions vs. Contract Sanctity

In "Abrogating Trade Contracts" (Op-Ed March 27), Representative Howard Berman argued against the contract sanctity amendment in the Senate version of the Export Administration Act, claiming that it would "deprive the Government of the valuable tool of trade sanctions."

The fact is, however, that trade sanctions rarely have proved to be effective tools of U.S. policy. They have been imposed to register opposition to foreign government policies or actions to which a diplomatic response seemed inadequate and a military response too dangerous. Unfortunately,

With Scot Marciel. Originally published in *The New York Times*, April 7, 1984. Used with permission of Michael R. Czinkota and *The New York Times*.

they have served more as symbols of U.S. discontent than as coercive or persuasive foreign policy instruments.

Perhaps trade sanctions are useful purely as symbols, but the benefits of symbolic protests need to be weighed carefully against their economic costs. Mr. Berman should realize that there is more at stake here than the "fulfillment of a particular company's export contract." Controls that force individual companies to break contracts also have damaging effects on overall export performance. With the U.S. facing a huge and growing trade deficit, this is no small matter.

The sanctions imposed by President Reagan against companies involved in the construction of the Soviet natural gas pipeline to Europe reflect the problems inherent in the use of foreign policy trade controls.

These sanctions surely symbolized U.S. opposition to the project, but they did not prevent its continuation. Meanwhile, they caused a great deal of harm to a number of U.S. and European companies. More important, they severely damaged the reputation of U.S. business in general.

Discussions with several foreign business executives and government officials following the U.S. embargo indicated that in the future they would think twice before entering into contracts with U.S. firms. One Latin American official asked: "Who knows who will be next on the U.S. hit list?"

If U.S. firms are to compete internationally, they must be guaranteed contract sanctity. The contract sanctity provision in the Senate bill will enhance the reputation of U.S. firms as reliable suppliers without diminishing the usefulness of foreign policy trade sanctions as symbolic protests. In fact, the provision may improve the effectiveness of sanctions because it will enable the U.S. Government to impose sanctions more easily and to maintain economic pressure for a longer period of time.

On Exports

International Export Control Systems Need Updating

Manufacturing competitiveness depends heavily on a government's application of export controls, which are a principal means of defending a nation's high technology advantage over potential adversaries.

In the United States, for example, it has been 23 years since the last major rewrite of the Export Administration Act (EAA), the legislation that provides the basic authority for the president to control exports. In the interim, U.S. practices have become ineffective and inefficient. Unless there is an update of the export control system, lack of coordination will decrease international manufacturing competitiveness.

With P. Freedenberg. Originally published in *Japan Today*, June 11, 2011. Used with permission of Michael R. Czinkota and *Japan Today*.

During the Cold War, the export controls of the U.S. and its allies successfully isolated the Soviet Union and denied—or at least delayed— its acquisition of the high technology necessary to strengthen its military.

Today, there is no longer unanimity among allies about the nature of the threats faced. Nor is there any longer a U.S. veto that can be wielded when there is disagreement. The current export control forum, the Was-senaar Group, is mostly concerned with keeping dangerous technology out of the hands of terrorists and rogue states.

However, some potential adversaries do not fit the Wassenaar Group profile. For example, China and Russia are certainly not rogue states, though the U.S. government retains a restrictive licensing policy towards them. In fact, the U.S. government is consistently more limiting than its European allies with regard to licenses for products and technologies des-tined for markets like China. Delays combined with foreign availability of products have meant lost business for U.S. firms and trade frictions with China.

Take, for example, China. It is the largest and fastest growing machine tool market in the world. The U.S. still tightly licenses five-axis machine tools, because they are considered to be the most sophisticated. U.S. export licenses can take from six months to a year to gain government approval. The Swiss, Germans and Italians readily take advantage of this delay by licensing products with identical capabilities in weeks. Over the past decade, the U.S. has lost 50% of its share in this fast-growing market, with domestic Chinese and foreign producers grabbing the lost market share. At the same time, the domestic U.S. market has shrunk by 50%. The effect on the United States defense industrial base has been predictably negative.

Similar problems have occurred in semiconductor manufacturing equipment and scientific instruments. Without the cooperation between allies, the export control system cannot work. It costs American jobs and does not accomplish its objectives.

The U.S. government may view China as a potential threat and seek to deny it the highest levels of technology, but many countries stand ready to supply China with whatever products and technology it wishes to acquire. The key issue is to develop an effective export control system that also receives support from other high technology exporting nations.

In the summer of 2009, President Barack Obama told his cabinet that he wanted to change export controls. The government is now working on reforms to provide a better definition of items on the military-oriented munitions list and those which constitute dual use technologies. Other reform plans deal with encryption, the mechanics of license processing, with speeding up licensing time and, most importantly, with shortening the list of products that require an individual validated license.

These reforms are a good first step. Export controls can be more relevant and effective if they are targeted and administered better. But more needs to be done by Congress in concert with the administration:

1. We need a better defined purpose for export controls, which our allies are willing to support.
2. We need to broaden the list of countries to which we have few or no controls, so that we can concentrate our efforts on rogue nations such as Iran and North Korea.
3. Export control implementation must be restructured. Combining and better defining the control lists should reduce endless interagency debates and shorten company waiting periods.

Our current system does not make sense for the 21st century. The president deserves strong congressional support in his efforts to harmonize and rationalize a licensing system that neither serves our national security nor our economic interests effectively. For the sake of a revitalized manufacturing sector, this is one of the few issues upon which both parties as well as the executive and legislative branches should be able to agree.

Doubling U.S. Exports: Can We Do It?

President Barack Obama has announced the goal of doubling U.S. exports within the next five years. Since the end of 2008, export growth has halted on a global level.

U.S. exports in 2009 were below those in 2007. Overall, in the 10 years from 2000, U.S. exports grew only by about 50 percent. Doubling exports in five years indicates a task four times as large, yet its achievement can greatly improve the economy and benefit American workers.

With C. Skuba. Originally published in the *Korea Times*, May 19, 2010. Used with permission of Michael R. Czinkota and the *Korea Times*.

How can we achieve such a goal? What activities need to be rebalanced or restructured to set us on the right path? How can, with prudent use of government resources, U.S. firms be enticed to export more?

With these kinds of questions in mind, we recently prepared testimony for the House Small Business Committee based on our extensive research on international business activity of U.S. companies.

Many U.S. businesses see only the risks of exporting rather than the opportunities of the international market. The psychological distance of foreign markets and uncertainties about international business practices are key barriers to many U.S. managers.

As a result, the United States under exports when compared to other nations. On a per capita basis, German exports in 2009 were $13,670 for every man, woman, and child. The figure for Japan was $4,063; for the United States, it was only $3,238.

When a firm starts to export, management's perception of risk exposure grows. There are entirely new factors such as currency exchange rates, greater distances, new modes of transportation, new government regulations, new legal and financial systems, new languages, and often substantial cultural diversity.

At the same time, due to investment needs into the exporting effort the immediate profit performance may deteriorate. Our research indicates that export procedural expertise is crucial for successful performance. Such expertise and managerial ability falls short even for experienced large exporters.

During the first two years of exporting, managers may face the unusual condition of rising risk accompanied by decreasing rewards. In light of this reality, and not knowing whether there will be a pot of gold at the end of the rainbow, many executives either do not initiate export activities or discontinue them.

There is a short-term gap in the working of market forces. Government export assistance can help firms over this rough patch to the point where profits increase again and risk heads downward. Bridging this short-term market gap may well be the key role of export assistance, and the major justification for the involvement of the public sector.

Export assistance can target the organizational characteristics and capabilities of the firm and improve them. It can also work on the managerial characteristics and contribute to knowledge and competence. Government also needs to continually monitor the environment and opportunities, as well as barriers, for U.S. companies.

Export assistance will be most effective when it reduces the risk to the firm and increases its rewards from export operations. For example, providing information on market potential abroad is likely to decrease the risk (both real and perceived) to the firm. Offering low-cost credit is likely to increase the rewards.

Export promotion is necessary. Here are some suggestions: Since exporting competence is crucial, the Department of Commerce could sponsor a professional certification in exporting to be taught in business schools and community colleges.

Liberal arts students should incorporate some international business education in their programs. Exporting must become a national game plan, just as it has been for decades in Japanese and German society and is now in China. The time is right for such an initiative.

States could rally annual competitions for the best case study written on an export entry success. Such studies should present an export problem which was solved.

Just like the peer reference power of adolescents, companies need concrete success stories they can read about to convince them that exporting is worth pursuing.

Such case work should involve support from the U.S. Commercial Service, Export Assistance Centers and Chambers of Commerce. Hundreds of short cases a year could be added to national resource centers. Available online, these cases could help in training swaths of interested people.

Congress might consider the development and implementation of an "Export Impact Statement" in connection with major policy decisions. Export trade considerations should also become an integral part of foreign policy negotiations instead of just an afterthought.

It must be recognized that successful international trade leads to a strong U.S. economy, which in turn is the necessary prerequisite for this country to remain the guarantor of its political achievements.

Finally, budget issues need to be considered. To be first class in international trade cannot be done on a shoestring. We need to invest in our export knowledge, processes and capabilities. The native American proverb says: "When storms come about, little birds seek to shelter, while eagles soar." We should help our exporters to become eagles.

Exporters Can Lead
Recovery

Just like his international counterparts, U.S. Commerce Secretary nominee Gary Locke has some depressing global economic data to confront as he prepares assuming the job of America's Chief Export Officer. There is little good news anywhere in the world on the trade front and 2009 does not hold much promise for export growth. However, trade data show that Mr. Locke may have good reason to encourage U.S. businesses to invest in future success overseas.

With C. Skuba. Originally published in the *Korea Times*, December 20, 2009. Used with permission of Michael R. Czinkota and the *Korea Times*.

As has been typical for the past three decades, global activities reflect, in an outsized way, the shifts in domestic economies. When domestic consumption is up, trade is up even more. Nowadays, when domestic activities are down, trade is down as well, only much more so. With predictions of further economic decline and contracting global demand, further international slides can be expected. Indeed, the release of annual trade data by the Commerce Department this month showed that U.S. exports declined six percent in December following a depressing November. Yet, a closer look at the trade data does offer some encouraging longer term implications.

First, the decline in the U.S. trade deficit, which hit a six-year low in December, was good news. The trade data reveal underlying strength in exports. Barring a steep rise in the price of oil imports, the decline in the trade deficit, which still stands at a daunting $678 billion for the year 2008, promises to continue. Imports are down more sharply than exports, despite their larger base. Economic theory, recent trends, and experience from previous cycles promise a continuation of that import decline and the one sided overhang in the bilateral trade balances.

American goods and services producers have continued to build demand among overseas customers. 2008 was a record year for U.S. exports which passed $1.8 trillion. Exports grew at a rate of 12 percent over 2007 and now comprise 13.1 percent of U.S. GDP. U.S. annual export growth has been in double digits from 2004 through 2008 and has outpaced import growth since 2006. Through mid-summer, this export growth had been sizzling along at a rate of nearly 19 percent before slowing as the global economy began to contract and Boeing workers went on strike.

In seven of the top ten export markets for the United States in 2008, American exports growth exceeded that of imports by nearly twice or more. U.S. exports to Mexico and China, our second and third largest export markets, grew at 11.4 percent and 9.5 percent while imports only grew at 2.5 percent and 5.1 percent respectively. Exports to Canada, the largest market, grew at 5 percent while imports grew slightly more at 5.8 percent, reflecting the interconnectedness of the two economies.

U.S. service providers have also demonstrated a strong growth pattern. In 2008, U.S. service exports grew faster than imports, interrupted only by the one-time payment, made in August, for the broadcast rights for the 2008 Summer Olympics. Overall, the U.S. services surplus increased $24.9 billion to an annual record of $144.1 billion.

We believe that American manufacturers and service firms are well positioned globally because they are increasingly delivering what the world prefers and wants. U.S. worker productivity in manufacturing continues to increase at a rate faster than most of the major competitor nations.

The reasons for eventual success are rooted in marketing factors. Decades of dedication to innovation, quality, customer-centrism, marketing research, and branding, is providing American companies with an advantage. As the 2008 Business Week annual ranking of the 100 Best Global Brands shows, even in difficult times, 52 of the leading brands were American.

Of course, when demand is down among the world's global trading partners, little or no trade growth is likely to occur until a recovery begins. However, it makes sense to prepare for when global buyers regain confidence. This applies to all nations. Many countries have export promotion capabilities and the expertise needed to help more of their firms market overseas. Our research shows that it typically takes new exporters about two years to get their international legs before they begin to realize good sales results. Our University currently sees a great increase in the applications for our MBA programs—since many students want to stock up on knowledge and capabilities during bad times in order to be ready for the good ones. Companies can do the same. Now is the time to use slack resources to explore new market opportunities, new cultures, new customers. Then, when economic conditions get better, companies can pounce on the markets they have researched and prepared for. Export promotion is a vital economic stimulus. Let's not lose time in supporting the international preparation of firms.

Exports: Its Business Not Government

Exports were mentioned in U.S. President Barack Obama's State of the Union address. Such U.S. presidential attention tends to be very special. However, there was virtually no focus on what needs to be done and how goals can be achieved. Though exports have no party affiliation, the policies leading to them do.

The U.S. economy needs a boost. Though the world may count on the U.S. import locomotive, this time around, U.S. exports need to have global priority. In the 10 years from 2000 to 2009, U.S. exports grew by about 50%. The president's goal to double U.S. exports by 2014 requires twice the increase in half the time. It's hard to generate trade momentum that quickly.

Originally published in *Japan Today*, February 4, 2011. Used with permission of Michael R. Czinkota and *Japan Today*.

Americans generally are quite good in working their way up to a leadership position. But since the 1980s, ongoing large and growing trade deficits have undermined its economic foundation. Just as one thinks about America as a nation of open skies and new opportunities, exports must become a national objective. Exports not only help an economy, but also allow the sharing of quality, choices and lower prices with the world.

Conditions and preparation matter. A company in Israel or Liechtenstein never questions whether or not to export. Their small home market makes exports a condition of survival. The literature calls those firms "born global." German exports in 2009 were $13,670 for every man, woman and child, while for the United States they were only $3,238. U.S. firms tend to focus on the substantial opportunities at home. But they need to recognize the export imperative as well.

U.S. consumers are wealthy and interested, and Americans are willing to give outsiders a chance. They enjoy trying a new product early and to exercise their right and capability to choose. This desire and capacity to innovate needs to be translated into the design and export of new goods and services.

Historically, U.S. trade policy has not been very helpful to exporters. Congress typically intervened by restricting, rather than liberalizing trade flows. Concerns mostly focused on helping other nations get their feet back on the ground. Now American managers need some better track shoes.

Today, exporters face new conditions. Technology has reduced global distance. The cultural diversity of America overcomes psychological distances between countries. Immigration brings expertise and encourages new business activities abroad. Increased knowledge reduces the burden of foreignness when going international.

Trade imbalances generate new export opportunities, sometimes of the two-faced Janus type. For example, the U.S. trade deficit makes it much cheaper to ship a container to Asia, than to bring one from there into the U.S. But a greater flow of goods to Asia will likely raise shipping prices. A lower dollar makes it easier to export, but also reduces U.S. purchasing power. There is little benefit to exporting if one receives little in return.

There is new interest in U.S. international business performances. The Korean Free Trade Agreement, the renewed negotiations with nations in international forums such as the World Trade Organization, and the just announced deal between the United States and China for $45 billion of U.S. exports provide impetus. But there needs to be much more. For example, given that China will need thousands of airplanes in the next decades, why not sign Boeing up for a much larger portion?

During the past 40 years, the largest U.S. trade growth was in imports—that's where the money was. For those looking to international markets today and tomorrow, the shoe is on the other foot—the exporters will have it. Now it is the U.S. turn to export—both a challenge and obligation to U.S. firms and government.

At the same time, trade distorting subsidies need to be curtailed. Exports need to be the result of capability and responsiveness to international needs. Our trading partners need to accept, that exports and imports do not happen in a vacuum. They are linked, and their desire for market preservation requires their interest in a strong U.S. economy, enhanced by U.S. exports.

History is characterized by non-linearity—not everything always keeps going the same way. Discontinuities and structural breaks herald new directions. Government attention to exports and imports needs to be streamlined and given a new priority. Just as ambassadors know to track and support policies abroad, trade need to become a new key concern for many. One could even envision an "export impact statement" for new regulations. We need a national export vision responsive to and expansive of U.S. capabilities. At this time, an American export avalanche may well happen in the long term, but only due to the new pioneers in business.

Exports and Imports for U.S. Manufacturers

U.S. manufacturing needs policy help, now. Low exports and a surge of imports have left the sector vulnerable, endangering future economic progress and hollowing out our defense industrial base.

Our trade deficits for goods with Mexico, Germany, Japan, and China are huge and getting bigger. Last year, the U.S. deficit with just China was $103 billion. We have an imbalance of $111 billion in motor vehicles alone. The imbalance is actually greater than even we can quantify, because there is no way to measure the amount of foreign parts in U.S.- exported goods.

U.S. firms clearly don't do enough exporting. It's not that they don't want to. There are simply too many bureaucratic obstacles for many of

With D. Manzullo Originally published in *The Washington Times*, May 27, 2003. Used with permission of Michael R. Czinkota and *The Washington Times*.

them to overcome. Compared to almost 34 percent for the European Union and 26 percent for China, U.S. exports pale, with only 11 percent of total gross domestic product. Almost half of all import shipments come from foreign affiliates, captive suppliers and U.S. subsidiaries.

The peril is apparent: When the manufacturing sector disappears, the effects go beyond lost jobs. Replacement parts become unavailable. Product re-orders take weeks rather than days. Do we really want to depend on old friends abroad for the rapid supply of manufactures critical to national security?

Manufacturing migration affects innovation and market responsiveness. By staying close to market and using emerging technologies in new products, companies gain experience and boost performance. When production is moved offshore, the rapid-response capability to market demands is dulled. A good example is what is happening with the SARS virus and its impact on global supply chains. The April 22, 2003 issue of *Investor's Business Daily states* "the threat of supply chain disruptions from China, Taiwan, Singapore and Indonesia is real… Computer, electronics, apparel and other firms are edgy about supply-chain troubles as their Asian partners send thousands of workers home and shut assembly lines."

When manufacturing firms close up shop, file for bankruptcy protection or move operations overseas, it's Americans who lose. We lose local expertise and strong competition. The once-demanding customers for American made products now become demanding customers for foreign-made goods.

Moving manufacturing overseas will also have other long-term consequences. A study at Temple University has found that the creation of new technology is a painstaking learning process of continual adjustment as new productive methods are tested. It is the small and medium manufacturers that create 55 percent of workplace innovations. The shifts abroad may eradicate technology and design and process advantages, placing U.S. firms and the country at further, future disadvantage.

Long-term economic adjustment does little for the unemployed overwhelmed by immediate needs. We don't think the answer is more legislation against countries and industries that account for substantial imbalances. That substitutes government judgment for market direction, which is not a very successful and sustainable replacement. Typically, prices rise disproportionately, consumers are deprived of desirable goods and firms find their ability to export undermined.

Policy must encourage existing market activities. Firms seeking export assistance should be supported by one personal export officer [PEXO], regardless of which agency handles the details. At our suggestion, the administration recently created an interagency training program to improve trade facilitation services for small businesses bewildered by the process and number of government forms, agencies, and participants. The Trade Promotion Coordinating Committee, composed of the 19 federal agencies that facilitate trade, conducted the first interagency seminar for PEXOs in January 2003.

There also needs to be more support for the fusion of goods, services and global networks. Consider how the automotive industry has combined airbags, the global positioning system and car telephones. Car manufacturers offer a new level of passenger assistance that can independently notify emergency services in case of an accident. Such fusions of readily available products are crucial to innovation.

Regulators should consider global implications. U.S. export control rules need to be precise and targeted, but not needlessly inhibiting to firms. Likewise, if a U.S. export order requires inspection by foreign buyers, visa regulations should flexibly accommodate the need for a brief visit.

But who pays for the adjustments? Currently, there is no link between governmental market openings and benefits obtained by an industry. Trade negotiations results in winners and losers, but winners have no incentive to share their bounty. The beneficiaries of protective measures do not show how they have used their revenues to help the transition of workers and communities. This must change. Private-sector winners must supplement the federal Trade Adjustment Assistance programs to help fund the cost of adjustment and become an essential engine for further trade liberalization. After all, even free trade has its price.

Commerce Secretary Locke Can Set Stage for Stronger Economic Recovery

Former Washington Gov. Gary Locke has some depressing economic data to confront as he prepares for the job of America's Chief Export Officer. There is little good news anywhere in the world on the trade front and 2009 does not promise export growth. However, reinforcing President Obama's confidence in American business "as the engine of growth," trade data show that, once confirmed, Commerce Secretary Locke has

With C. Skuba Originally published in *The Seattle Times*, March 6, 2009. Used with permission of Michael R. Czinkota and *The Seattle Times*.

good reason to lead the charge in encouraging U.S. businesses to invest in future success overseas thus creating jobs at home.

As has been typical for the past three decades, global activities reflect, in an outsized way, the shifts in the domestic economy. When domestic consumption is up, trade is up even more. Nowadays, when domestic activities are down, trade is down as well, only much more so. With expected economic decline in 2009 and contracting global demand, further international slides are probable. The release of annual trade data by the Commerce Department last month showed U.S. exports declined 6 percent in December following a depressing November. Yet, a look at the trade data offers encouraging longer-term implications for U.S. exporters and the workers they employ.

First, the decline in the U.S. trade deficit, which hit a six-year low in December, was good news. The trade data reveal underlying strength in U.S. exports. Barring a steep rise in the price of oil imports, the decline in the trade deficit, which stands at a daunting $678 billion for the year 2008, promises to continue. Imports are down more sharply than exports, despite their larger base. Economic theory, recent trends, and experience from previous cycles promise a continuation of that import decline. Any import growth in 2008 was attributable to the high price of petroleum products.

On the export side, American goods and services have continued to build demand among overseas customers. 2008 was a record year for U.S. exports, which passed $1.8 trillion. Exports grew at a rate of 12 percent over 2007 and now comprise 13.1 percent of U.S. GDP. This marks a continuing trend, since U.S. annual export growth has been in double digits from 2004 through 2008 and has outpaced import growth since 2006. Through mid-summer, U.S. export growth had been sizzling along at a rate of nearly 19 percent before slowing as the global economy began to contract and Boeing workers went on strike.

In seven of the top 10 export markets for the United States in 2008, American exports growth exceeded that of imports by nearly twice or more. U.S. exports to Mexico and China, our second- and third-largest export markets, grew at 11.4 percent and 9.5 percent, respectively, while imports only grew at 2.5 percent and 5.1 percent. Exports to Canada, our largest market, grew at 5 percent while imports grew slightly more at 5.8 percent, reflecting the interconnectedness of the two economies.

Trade liberalization has been a significant reason. The U.S. merchandise trade deficit with free-trade-agreement (FTA) partner countries narrowed by $16 billion, while the deficit with the non-FTA countries increased by $22 billion. In 2008, the United States actually had a trade surplus in manufactured goods of $17 billion with the 14 countries with which it had an FTA in effect. Free trade agreements work!

Equally important is also the fundamental fact that American manufacturers and service providers are increasingly delivering what the world prefers and wants. American companies have a good competitive position globally because of a decades-in-the-making dedication to improved productivity, innovation, quality, customer-centrism, marketing research and branding. When global buyers regain confidence, American brands can be confident.

So, what can Commerce Secretary Locke do to support the growth track of exports?

For one thing, given the advantages free-trade agreements bring to American exporters, he should be a champion for Congressional passage of pending agreements with Colombia, Panama and Korea. These agreements would give a much-needed shot-in-the-arm during this difficult economic stretch as they would lessen the current uneven tariff burden for U.S. companies in these markets. There are no fundamental obstacles to the Panama FTA. With Colombia, there are paths forward to help resolve Congressional reservations over the issues of violence against labor leaders and related criminal impunity. The Korean FTA presents a bigger challenge in Congress but it would also bring a bigger economic reward.

But, more immediately, Locke needs to ensure funding and commitment for export-promotion efforts. The Commerce Department's International Trade Administration has a powerful export-promotion capability all around the world and the expertise needed to help more American companies sell overseas. The timing is right. Our research shows that it takes new exporters about two years to get their international legs before they begin to realize good sales results. Just as our university sees a great increase in the applications for our MBA program—since many students want to stock up on knowledge and capabilities during bad times, companies can do the same.

Now is the time to use slack resources to explore new market opportunities, new cultures and new customers. Then, when economic conditions get better, companies can pounce on the markets they have researched and prepared for. Export promotion is a vital economic stimulus. Let's not lose time in applying the government capabilities to support our firms.

On Education

Universities Must Embrace Cultural Change

Universities are among the most successful institutions created. But what role do universities need to play in the knowledge society of tomorrow to continue their success? This question grows more pressing for the western welfare states, as their dominance in research and innovation is being challenged by globalisation and the dynamics of the emerging economies.

The example of the US, which like no other nation, has been able to benefit from universities as drivers of growth, makes this abundantly clear. For a long time America has combined cutting-edge university research

With A. Pinkwart. Originally published in the *Financial Times*, August 15, 2011. Used with permission of Michael R. Czinkota and the *Financial Times*.

with strong science and engineering and entrepreneurial-oriented business schools. This has allowed the country to promote groundbreaking innovations.

Yet, in an era of major shifts in information flows and communication practices, there are increasing doubts about whether the concepts that allowed previous innovations remain sympathetic to the challenges and research priorities of the future.

The advance of biotechnology and social sciences absorbs almost half the research funds of US universities. Add the expansion of national security and military research, and universities have lost important drivers for the industrial use of new scientific insights. Instead, the ivory towers, which were once believed to have been abandoned, have re-emerged. Tackling the gigantic US budget deficit, will also require new structures and processes in research and teaching at universities.

In Europe, Germany may appear to be in better shape to innovate, with its broad mix of industrial and service-related leadership and its strong and flexible small and medium-sized businesses. However, this should not obscure obvious weaknesses. What has been achieved through a drive for excellence and high-tech initiatives, for which the government has provided competitive university funding and more autonomy in recent years, may be lost once more. Ideological campaigns declare either that universities are not and should not be subject to economic rules, or express fears about standardised expectations, which are said to lead to a commoditisation of higher education.

Universities must deliver on accepted performance measures yet differentiate themselves sufficiently to attract scarce resources under competitive conditions.

Germany and the US face similar problems. So far the American and the German university system have learnt from each other in a time-delayed fashion. Now, due to mounting competitive and financial pressures, universities need to learn from each other simultaneously. University success is not about tearing down the ivory towers. Instead, it is about opening their windows as far as possible to other disciplines and to new markets.

While freedom of teaching and research must be defended, at the same time bridges for mutual transfers of knowledge and best practices have to be built.

We need Alexander von Humboldt's ideas to be applied to the 21st century. The university of the future is only viable if best research and best teaching go hand in hand with best knowledge transfers. To achieve these goals, universities need reliable funding to generate innovative ideas through research. Interdisciplinary links, a close integration with the environment (both social and natural) as well as research relevance are also necessary.

All this calls for a major cultural change on both sides of the Atlantic. For new scientific knowledge to be used more rapidly in universities and businesses, the university approach to knowledge generation, transmission and application needs to be rethought. More risk capital, new business models and efficient intermediary organisations are needed in order to build a bridge over the valley of death, in which so many basic research contributions have perished before they could become innovations.

Such efforts would be worthwhile. It is not only about wealth and employment; it is also about the development opportunities of each individual and the defence of intellectual freedom.

A New Era for Universities

Universities and their internationalization are important. Traditional knowledge exporters, such as the United States, Germany, France and England, aim to maintain their high share in the growing international academic market. They recognize the economic benefits of educating students who, when back home, will decide about purchases for infrastructure, engineering and other economic goals.

Exporting higher education generates income for universities and encourages them to become global entrepreneurs. The market is growing. Higher education students have increased by 53% since 2000 to more than 150 million in 2007. In Australia and New Zealand, education is

With A. Pinkwart. Originally published in the *Korea Times*, May 23, 2011. Used with permission of Michael R. Czinkota and the *Korea Times*.

the third and fourth ranking services export. In the United States, international students and their dependents contributed $18.8 billion to the economy during the 2009–2010 academic year.

Universities shift their role from a provider of human resources to an innovation engine and entrepreneurial hub. Academic knowledge is transferred to new products and processes. Due to its ability to integrate international students and researchers, academia can commercialize knowledge and research in ways that companies cannot replicate.

Traditional internationalization within universities was a bottom-up activity, based on personal connections by an individual faculty member or by research teams. Increasingly, however, leading universities grow internationally as part of a top-down activity driven by institutional directives. Several key reasons account for this shift: A scientific approach demands awareness of and interaction with international work in order to benchmark one's own competence. Internationalization is also part of becoming a competitive enterprise and contributes to capacity utilization. As part of their mission, universities need to provide a global social infrastructure and networks for their graduates. They also can assume new roles as incubators and connectors for emerging ideas and innovations. Asian countries in particular undertake major efforts to enhance the position of their universities.

For centuries, universities were leaders in international activities. They exported and imported students and faculty members by either admitting them or by sending them abroad. Latin as the lingua franca facilitated exchanges of personnel. New locations were sought out, and international partnerships helped expansion, or were a means to escape poor conditions. For example, Georgetown University, a Jesuit school in Washington DC, was left in legal limbo in the late 18th century, when pope Clement XIV suppressed the Jesuit order. However, by working with Jesuits in Byelorussia, the order continued to be recognized by Czarina Katherine the Great. For several decades, the Georgetown Jesuits were members of the Russian Province. Universities also raised funds on an international scale. They ensured international quality control, when in 1233 A.D. a papal bull ordered that those admitted as teachers in Toulouse, had the right to teach anywhere without further examinations.

Today, companies are the international leaders. They differentiate their international activities into investments (inflow and outflow) and trade (imports and exports). They shift entry approaches based on market needs. To some markets they export. Global sourcing and offshoring is used in others. Firms conduct franchising or licensing and often recruit their staff from around the globe. They make investments, either as sole owners or in joint ventures, and shift venues whenever necessary.

Universities have limited their response to globalization. Typically, they do not translate their experience into an institutional strategy. Many exchange programs do not outlive their faculty founders. International hiring decisions are mostly made in isolation rather than as part of a planned direction. Research collaborations tend to be temporary and international investments have been very limited—be it due to budget or risk constraints.

Since the 1980's, globalization has moved university activities towards the market. Though universities are the prototype of knowledge institutions, there is only a very limited body of internationalization research in this important service sector. Experience is insufficiently recorded and not remembered. Insights tend to be peer reviewed based on academic criteria, with scant links to constituency needs. In consequence the knowledge and guideposts on internationalization is thin, and constitutes for many universities merely a search for student markets or respect among colleagues. International partnerships often only are intriguing wallpaper for a university president's office. University implementation of international strategy often remains at the level of international business activities by smaller and medium sized businesses: limited, ad-hoc, unsystematic and frequently inconsistent.

Universities need to demonstrate the international benefits they can offer. The Roman Empire mainly expanded by offering market places, roads, language, laws, and linkages. Outsiders joined because affiliation offered the opportunity to live better. Universities need to achieve such voluntary interest as well. Given their knowledge base, their human talent and their cross-disciplinary capabilities, universities need to make the cost of non-collaboration so high that firms seek them out as knowledge source and partner. In addition to funding, universities need freedom. Just as universities helped define the openness and knowledge of principalities and kingdoms, today they can help define global society, competitiveness and influence.

In developing content, universities should concentrate on specific aspects in which to become multidisciplinary experts. Specialization has worked for firms, and will allow universities to provide more value added to society. It will also be important to provide the connectivity between business, research and policy. Profits alone are insufficient for societal prosperity. Religion, family, culture, security are only a few of the components which universities can incorporate a systemic perspective. This will set their thinking apart and lets their educational efforts become the transmission belt for the internationalization of their economy.

Too Soon to Let Computers Replace University Libraries

The University of Texas (UT) at Houston has announced that it is removing almost all the books from its undergraduate library to provide space for a digital learning center, where students can use computers to access a wide variety of information. University officials are proud to be leading a trend.

It is good to see academia catching up with technology.

But what are the repercussions of this shift? I am thinking about this from various perspectives:

Teacher, researcher, author and reader.

Originally published in *The Japan Times*, May 25, 2005. Used with permission of Michael R. Czinkota and *The Japan Times*.

When I became a doctoral student, my department chairman sent me a list of 45 books for the summer before my studies commenced. Initially I thought of picking one or two favorite titles, but a telephone call clarified the issue: I was to read every single book, and discuss them intelligently in our seminar. So I made sure that I had prescription sunglasses and went to work!

Today, whenever I assign two chapters of a book to my students for our next meeting, I get requests for clarification. I know that I am becoming outdated in my reading demands and the removal of books at UT will only hasten the demise of my apparently tyrannosaurical expectations.

We use books to learn what others before us have thought—which forms the basis for our research. But do we really need books for that? Much research requires persistence, perseverance and perspiration to carry out repetitive organizational tasks that develop our understanding of a field. Computers are quite well equipped to help with such chores. They allow us to manipulate, search, collate, extract, compare—something that only vandals can do with books. Yet, is our understanding weaker because of changes in the process?

Sources and citations used to be a scholar's stock in trade, but just like the grinding skills of lens crafters, these talents are not much sought after anymore today—machines are so much better at it. By going to Google Scholar one can find citations typically in 0.4 second or less. My students barely cite "hard" copies of journals anymore; their reference sections come from the Web.

Yet, Web research places an awesome responsibility on scholars and their search engines. How do we avoid the thinking that if something does not show up on a computer search it simply does not exist? How do we steer clear of consigning writings into oblivion just because they are either less recent or not in English, or not cited often enough?

Will such practices permanently affect our capacity to innovate and to spread new thought or will we create a reader's "Mayan" syndrome where later generations will wonder why we abandoned existing knowledge?

As a writer of books, their removal from libraries saddens me. But textbooks can cost more than $100 today, a price at which publishers are telling me that they barely can survive. By contrast, a CD with dynamite programs that allow interactivity offer wonderful colors and online work, weighs very little, and costs only a fraction of a book. Yet payments for software and online activities are not as well worked out as they are for books; illegal downloads are rampant.

Many CDs are actual adaptations of existing books. We have publishers unwilling to invest, authors who may know their content but are not computer experts and a market where compensation is uncertain. These factors raise questions about who will make the effort to write the new texts, who will review them for quality and who will publish them?

Finally, some thoughts from a reader's perspective. To me, books feel good. Reading aloud with my daughter and turning a page is special. Seeing a book again after many years is like running into an old friend—it brings back memories, and helps me make a connection between temporal distances. When visiting someone I always like to glance at the books. A look at their "holdings" gives me a good sense of what we share, what we can talk about and what direction any future relationship would take.

So here we are. Time marches on relentlessly and perhaps this is the dawn of a new era. Johannes Gensfleisch Gutenberg and his invention of the printing press have had a good run. The Texans may know best when to fold them and when to walk away, but at the current state of the art I think books will be with us for a while yet. The person you see at the beach reading in the breeze and not worrying about moisture or grains of sand may well be me. Feel free to set up your computer!

Academic Freedom for All

Academic freedom is close to the hearts of many. Being able to teach what "needs" to be taught, to speak out and to pursue thoughts to wherever they may lead are some of the most crucial components of academia. In light of this accepted axiom it is surprising to learn about opposition to the free exercise of higher education around the world.

Soon the World Trade Organization will take up the discussion of liberalizing cross-border services as part of the Doha Round. In an era of the knowledge society, one would expect negotiators to support the free flow of higher education across national borders. To the contrary, there is substantial resistance to the integration of this sector into the General Agreement on Trade in Services (GATS). Only four of 148 WTO members have suggested more openness.

Many countries are held back by vigorous resistance from their own universities. In their Statement on Behalf of Higher Education

Originally published in *The Japan Times*, April 23, 2005. Used with permission of Michael R. Czinkota and *The Japan Times*.

Institutions Worldwide, university associations from around the world proclaim fundamental disagreement with international competition: "Trade frameworks are not designed to deal with the academic, research, or broader social and cultural purposes of higher education."

There are several reasons why universities don't want open markets for themselves. First is the reluctance to accept a role in an existing global framework. Administrators and professors around the world have consistently assured me that university issues are so special, specific and unique that the application of industry approaches to them would be heresy. As the editor of an important business journal put it, "Reviewers generally reject the notion that higher education is a 'service.'"

Second is an overwhelming unwillingness by universities in most nations to consider the benefits of an entrepreneurial system. Typically, funding comes from the government, salaries are set based on years of service and grants are awarded based on seniority. Rewards for university management come for the ability to manage coalitions and increase subsidies, rather than the capacity to raise funds or be market responsive. There are very few rewards for academic process innovation.

Third is an ingrained opposition to competition and market forces. Little confidence exists in the power of the market to assure quality. To the world, the evidence is quite clear that central planning has not worked. Yet for ideological and historical reasons, many universities around the globe remain the last vestiges of central planning.

Past centuries have seen few shifts in university structures and processes. If we could time-transport a Heidelberg professor from 1386 to one of today's universities, that person would be a fully functional professional. There still is the classroom with the cathedra from which the professor expounds great thoughts and the seats from which students claim to listen. There still are the volumes to read, the papers to write and the ritualized exams to take. Mostly, one professor still offers only one field at one university, and students still receive their knowledge in one-course increments which, as if by magic, last exactly one semester, and obtain their degrees from only one location.

All this in an era characterized by technology-driven knowledge generation and information dissemination, global reach, cross fertilization of fields, substantial productivity enhancements and Six Sigma quality-control levels. It might appear as if higher education has not innovated at the same pace as other industries.

Where other sectors have used advances in telecommunications, technology, and ease of border crossing to make important progress in productivity, academia continues to increase expenses per student without improved returns. On this road, the academic industry will either decline into mass institutions of little value or offer higher education only for a select few.

Universities need more funding, more competition and more insights from around the globe. Student mobility around the world needs to be reinvigorated. Professors and researchers should move about more. Program content should be internationalized with increasing ease through distance learning and online education. Universities should be able to open up branches abroad or join forces with foreign entities. Competition for resources and students between the best institutions with a minimum of governmental inhibitions must let ventures succeed or fail. This, however, will only happen if GATS rules apply to the academic sector.

Advanced nations perhaps have to accommodate too many entrenched forces to achieve academic liberalization rapidly. The emerging nations, many of which have been excluded from the benefits of higher education, can achieve the greatest gains from global university liberalization. We should advocate the application of WTO rules now to cause improvements in academia to happen quickly and widely around the world.

Decline in the Factories
of Academe

This is the tale of an industry in a battle for survival. Its firms had experienced tremendous growth until the 1980s. Government had subsidized industry expansion. New plants shot up all over the country. Its products were popular. Its managers and employees did not receive the highest wages, but there were long vacations and a generous employee discount. Similar to Japanese practices, lifetime employment was guaranteed for most employees. Comparable to Sweden, a very loosely structured, self-motivated job environment was offered.

Originally published in the *Chicago Tribune*, March 6, 1990. Used with permission of Michael R. Czinkota and the *Chicago Tribune*.

Today a sour note begins to be heard in that industry. The client base shrinks. Prices have risen tremendously. Former customer groups are priced out of the market. Terms of sale lack transparency. There is overproduction of certain products, and quality control concerns have arisen. Productivity growth is virtually nonexistent, and there is a clamor for more public subsidy. Much effort is expended on investigating the maladies of the industry. Blue-ribbon panels and conferences are convened; the government launches support programs. But still the industry remains in decline.

This is not the steel or the semiconductor industry. It is our university industry. The tragic part of the above description is that most universities have yet to realize the perilous road of decline, and the industry as a whole has yet to take major steps to pull back from the abyss.

Even though universities should question everything under the sun, they do not have a good record of questioning themselves. From a productivity viewpoint, universities teach in the ways of Paris or Bologna in the 12th Century-professors gather the students around and lecture. Instructors employ textbooks as primary tools, invented by Gutenberg in 1450. Productivity increases mean larger classes or teaching with lower-priced faculty. Innovation means launching a new course-after years of faculty debate.

All of this starkly resembles the re-arranging of deck chairs on the Titanic. Universities are working hard on improving the way they build horse buggies, but fail to notice that the world is driving cars. What happened to the application of modern technology to the teaching industry? Where is the integration of innovations in telecommunications? Where is the use of market research? Who focuses on the principle of comparative advantage?

Take textbooks. The author writes from three to six years on a text. The review by colleagues and editing takes another year. Add one more year for the production and marketing of the finished book, which will then remain on the market about four years. This means students will learn from a product whose information content is five to 12 years old. The product costs about $50 and is nothing like Nintendo. What a way to run a show nowadays.

Take introductory courses. In a university setting, they are the most crucial ones, since they have to transmit all the knowledge some students will ever be exposed to in a particular field, and steer others into majoring in the field. Is there really a need to conduct these courses in a classroom with a professor? Shouldn't it be possible to offer them with videotapes featuring the best professors from around the country complemented with computer-aided instruction? Or couldn't the existing technology of downlink and uplink instruction be used to provide interactive television courses? (Corporations do it all the time.)

In the meantime, tuition keeps going up, and education is becoming more elitist. Yes, we have an industry in decline. But just as government subsidies and price hikes did not help our steel mills, they will not improve the university landscape. The time has come to ask some other hard questions:

Are more courses needed or can mass education be replaced by niche education consisting of interchangeable modules tailored to each student's needs? Do exams have to be given? If yes, must they be given at a common site or can everybody fax theirs in? Do we need a summer break? Is there still a need for subdividing universities into departments or colleges?

Should universities collaborate more with firms and institutions-which are spending tens of billions on in-house training? Do we need professors to operate as administrators? Are teaching and research really inseparable? How can universities consciously maintain and even improve their socialization activities in the "campus" of the future?

Finding the answers is tough. To show results, however, we have to wake up and do something before another basic industry goes to the dogs.

Teaching People How
to Manage Change

Ours is a world in transition. The current global debate centers on the state of knowledge that led to the Iraq war. Neglected is the much more important discussion of the knowledge needed to bringing peace and prosperity to the world. The education sector can play a major role in teaching how to implement change around the globe.

There is a formidable need for administering national transition. Often soldiers are thrust into the roles of police officers, politicians,

Originally published in *The Japan Times*, October 13, 2003. Used with permission of Michael R. Czinkota and *The Japan Times*.

mayors and heads of public works. Most of them are not trained for such duties. Yet the need for their work continues to grow.

Think about the nations in the Middle East that need help. There are many Asian countries requiring assistance. One can also expect important transitions on the African continent.

Universities have internationalized over time but have not kept pace with globalization and the transformation of world relations. For many years foreign language training was the main international activity on campus. Over time, culture was added to the verbs, and international studies departments were formed. Policy concerns led to programs in international diplomacy.

More recently, global marketing and management courses have produced the now highly competitive international business programs. In all instances, however, little has been done to integrate the components that make up a society in order to deal with the conflicts and problems of transition management.

The time is now to create education programs with graduates who can coordinate such transitions on a global level. Let's forget about the notion of academic departmental silos and move beyond addressing problems in the isolation of research boundaries. Changing the culture of a country, achieving a transition to a market economy, integrating a country into the global family of nations are not tasks to be divided up by discipline.

New graduates must be grounded in democracy. They must know about the impact of culture and the workings of legal institutions. They need to have a sense of history and appreciation of ethics. They must be able to screen civil servants and determine who goes and who stays. They have to be able to administer crowd control, guard national treasures and provide for public health.

They will need to have an understanding of logistics and be experts at liaison with groups ranging from religious leaders to local zealots or representatives of international organizations. They will need to learn a dose of market-based thinking, but also be understanding of the importance of family ties.

Above all, they need to communicate well, convey a sense of hope, and be able to initiate a joint national purpose. A full palette indeed!

It will not be easy to pull together all the necessary capabilities to teach pacification and conciliation. Fortunately, there is a vast array of technology available to collect knowledge and to disseminate it. We can contact individuals at virtually any place in the world to obtain their insights. We can place at their disposal media tools that permit them to explain their views in the best possible way. We can provide for color, data transfer, group interaction, live views and taped lectures.

We can then use the same technology to reach out to the world and let a wide variety of students learn.

The main value of experience comes from preparing us for the future and helping us to avoid the repetition of mistakes. Now that we are exposed to the lessons in the field, we must observe and record what works and what doesn't. Learning and advancement will occur only if we codify that information into knowledge and then systematically communicate that knowledge.

This is the time to create a new level of thinking in academia. We must pool the best of knowledge, the most spirited desire for change and the deepest experience in implementation. Matching such an environment with the most talented students from around the world should give new meaning to the term "elite."

The locations for such learning need to be well connected to centers of power. It also helps to have the occasional physical presence of key decision makers from legislative and judicial bodies, military leaders and business executives for a hands-on knowledge transfer.

After all the sacrifices required to initiate change, we cannot afford to lose out on the long-term results just because people's minds and hearts are not won. Learning how to administer change is just as important as the initiation of change. The global education sector must step up to deliver what today's new world conditions require.

Here is the opportunity for a new coalition of many countries to provide the resources and knowledge for teaching how to do things better in the future.

Buying Education with Third World Debt

A Novel Idea from the U.S. Commerce Department

An innovative program that would increase the number of U.S. students studying in the Third World has been proposed by Michael Czinkota,

Originally published in *International Education Magazine*, May/June 1989. Used with permission of Michael R. Czinkota and *International Education Magazine*.

Deputy Assistant Secretary for Trade and Information Analysis of the U.S. Department of Commerce.

In his report, *Improving U.S. Competitiveness: Swapping Debt for Education,* Czinkota outlines how the Third World debt held by U.S. banks could be used to finance study abroad programs for American students in the debtor nations. Besides directly benefiting U.S. financial and educational institutions, the program is designed to strengthen the United States' position in international trade and business by improving competence in international matters among the nation's students.

The Debt Problem and the Baker Plan

The external debt of third-world countries with serious debt-servicing difficulties remains massive. The foreign obligations of the "Baker-15 countries" alone totalled about $460 billion at end-1986. $277 billion was owed to commercial banks, including $86 billion to U.S. banks.[1]

Administration strategy for dealing with LDC debt problems is contained in the Baker plan, which was unveiled in 1985. The main elements of the plan consist of increased lending to debtor LDCs by commercial banks and multilateral lending agencies—mainly the IMF and World Bank—in conjuction with adoption by the borrowing countries of market oriented reforms aimed at promoting growth and balance of payments equilibrium. The plan stresses the need for a case-by-case approach—that is, adapting lending reform packages to the individual circumstances of each debtor country. In this connection, the plan attaches great importance to the "menu" approach—that is, to the development by the banks of a wide range of lending options and devices to suit the needs and desires of both creditors and debtors.

Among the items that the Administration has recommended be placed on the menu is "donation of debt paper to charitable organizations for social and environmental uses in debtor nations."[2]

---

1. The countries are Argentina, Bolivia, Brazil, Chile, Colombia, Ecuador, Ivory Coast, Mexico, Morocco, Nigeria, Peru, Philippines, Uruguay, Venezuela, and Yugoslavia. These are the 15 nations to which the Baker plan is to be applied.

2. See text of "Remarks by Secretary of the Treasury James A. Baker, III to the Bretton Woods Committee Annual Meeting, Washington, D.C., Tuesday, February 16, 1988," p. 7, *Treasury News,* Department of the Treasury, Washington, D.C.

The Administration has thus given its blessing to innovative debt-reducing actions of a socially useful nature, one of which could be education. In fact, the easing of the LDC debt burden from charitable projects is likely to be marginal. But the social value of the projects in the beneficiary countries can be sizable.

To date, the charitable uses of LDC debt have been concentrated on conservation and environmental protection. For example, in mid-1987 a U.S. nonprofit organization purchased $650,000 of Bolivia's external debt in the open market for $100,000—a discount of 85 percent—and then cancelled the $650,000 obligation in exchange for a Bolivian promise "to give maximum legal protection to the Beni Biosphere Reserve and to increase by 3.7 million acres...the protected area next to the reserve."

Using Debt to Help Meet International Education Needs

...It would appear that a fairly large-scale program could be conducted with a relatively small amount of LDC debt. Some illustrative—indeed, impressionistic—figures suggest reasonable orders of magnitude. According to an estimate of one university business school professor thoroughly familiar with U.S. study-abroad programs, the average monthly cost of maintaining an American student in a third-world country is about $500.[3]

Thus the amount of LDC debt needed to pay the living expenses for a full year of 2,500 American students in the Baker plan countries would be about $15 million. (As noted above, about 2,500 American students received credit for study in these 15 countries in 1986.) Tuition payments to local universities—or capital and current expenditures for building and running study centers, if that option were chosen—would significantly raise the cost. But even if annual outlays per student were to run $20,000 a year—an improbably high figure—the annual cost for 2,500 students,

---

3. Business executives studying in third-world countries would be unlikely to be willing to live on $500 a month. However, presumably the companies for which they work would be expected to contribute to their expenses as part of the investment in their training.

at $50 million, would still be a minuscule fraction of the approximately $90 billion in Baker-plan-country debt held by U.S. banks. Furthermore, such an investment would double the current number of U.S. students in the Baker-15 countries....

Mechanisms and Procedures

Commercial banks can, if they choose, either donate or sell their holdings of LDC debt. Because of the current and likely on-going inability of many debtor countries to meet their debt-servicing obligations, banks may be motivated to take either or both of these actions as a way of cutting their losses. The price at which these loans are sold in free secondary markets is generally far below their face value—a reflection of the assessment in financial markets that these loans will never be fully serviced or repaid... A bank may also want to shed its LDC loans to extract itself from involuntary lending arrangements that require it to contribute to new loans packages to an LDC in proportion to its share of total outstanding bank loans to the LDC.

The Internal Revenue Service took action last year to increase the incentive to donate rather than sell debt. Under a ruling the IRS issued in November 1987–Rev. Rul. 87–124—a bank, through a donation process, may achieve a tax deduction on the full face value of its loan rather than on the loan's "fair market value" only. Previously, deductions were only allowed for the "fair market value" of the loan, that is on the discounted market price at which the loan could actually be sold. 87–124 in effect said that a bank could sell a loan to a foreign central bank for local currency, claim a tax deductible loss on the difference between the face value of the loan and the dollar value of the loan as measured by the amount of local currency it received for it, contribute the local currency it received to a U.S. charitable organization, and claim a tax deduction on the contribution.

However, even with the liberal treatment of donations under 87–124, a bank is still better off—other things being equal—if it sells the loan. That way it can claim a loss on the difference between the face value of the loan and the price it actually receives for it and pocket the full amount of the proceeds of the sale. To give an illustrative example: A U.S. bank donates a $1,000,000 loan—to a charitable organization. Assume the bank sells the loan at a 58 percent discount. It thus receives in local currency the equivalent of 42 percent of the face value of the loan in dollars. The bank thus can claim a tax deductible loss of $580,000–58 percent of the face value of the loan. The bank then donates the local currency it received to the charitable organization and can claim a tax deduction on a $420,000 charitable organization contribution. Thus the bank can claim tax deductions on the full $1,000,000. If the tax rate were 40 percent, it would save $400,000. Now assume that, instead of donating the land, it sells it in the free market at a 58 percent discount for $420,000. It claims a tax deductible loss of $580,000. It thus cuts its tax bill by $232,000 *and* has $420,000 in cash from the sale of the loan. Thus by selling the loan, it is better off, having "gained" $652,000, considerably more than $400,000.

This is not to say that a bank will never donate a loan. Donations may sometimes have significant advantages. For example, a donation might win public good will or be less embarrassing than an out-and-out write-off. Furthermore, on occasion, a bank may find that there is no market for one of its LDC loans. But donations are more likely to be the exception than the rule.

The most frequent technique for channelling LDC debt into charitable uses is for a U.S. charitable (or nonprofit) organization to buy the LDC debt from a bank at the market price and then exchange it for local currency in the LDC at a more favourable rate. For example, assume that, at the official exchange rate, one U.S. dollar is worth 10 units of Country X's currency, the peso. Assume that a U.S. bank disposes of a $1,000,000 loan to Country X at a 60 percent discount by selling it to a U.S. charitable organization for $400,000. Now assume that the U.S. charitable organization, which with the approval of Country X's government plans to spend local currency to establish a language training institute in Country X, negotiates an exchange of the loan, whose face value is still $1,000,000, for 8,000,000 pesos. (The rate at which a charitable organization exchanges dollars for local currency with the LDC government is always open to negotiation). The charitable organization is getting less than the official exchange rate. But it still comes out ahead, since—measured in terms of the official exchange rate—it has received

$800,000 worth of pesos for an expenditure of $400,000. In other words, the charitable organization did twice as well by following the procedure thus described than it would have had it bought pesos directly at the official exchange rate. What made it possible for the charitable organization to achieve this advantageous arrangement was the steep discount at which the bank was willing to sell its loan to Country X.

There are other ways that charitable organizations can obtain local currency to carry out their projects. In some cases, a charitable organization may be able to link up with a U.S. company that is involved in a debt-equity swap. Take the following example: U.S. firm F has bought a $1,000,000 loan to Country X from a U.S. bank. F now negotiates to exchange the $1,000,000 loan for 8,000,000 pesos that it will invest in an enterprise in Country X. At this point, University U, which wants to build a 1,000,000 peso language training centre in Country X that Country X fully approves of, approaches F. It informs F that U can arrange for F to receive 9,000,000 instead of 8,000,000 pesos for the $1,000,000 loan. F agrees to this arrangement. If F will donate 1,000,000 pesos to U and provide U's project with certain services, all parties benefit. U gets the money to build the language training centre. X gets the benefit of the centre. And F gets a tax deduction on its 1,000,000 peso contribution to U that presumably exceeds the value of the services it will provide U.

…In carrying out a debt-for-education program aimed at improving U.S. competitiveness, several main points need to be kept in mind.

- If LDCs are going to be receptive to the program, the projects proposed will have to be designed to contribute to the development of the host countries. Using local currency simply to place U.S. students in local universities or to send trade missions to a country may be considered insufficient by LDCs. There must also be major benefits for the host country.
- Education programs have been funded with blocked or specially designated funds in the past (e.g. Fulbright scholarships).
- The key for the success of a debt for education swap will be the participation and interest of the private sector. University and debt holders' enthusiasm is essential. Programs which

offer benefits to debt holders both in the U.S. and abroad are, therefore, more likely to attract funding.

– Despite a common financial underpinning, programs need not and should not be standardized, but rather be tailored to the educational needs and opportunities of participating institutions and countries.

– Debt swapping operations are complex and require substantial negotiations. In order for such transactions to be carried out successfully, the establishment of a clearing-house which benefits from the assistance of experienced professionals is necessary.

– The payoff of such a program in terms of competitiveness will not be immediate—yet it is imperative to start the educational process now to reap the rewards in the future.

On Thinking Ahead

Where Is the German Vision

When German Chancellor Gerhard Schroeder precipitated early elections in Germany, the decision to seek electoral guidance appeared appealing. Since then, the choices on Sept. 18 have been remarkable mainly for their paucity and obscurity. Unless the parties and their candidates are able to crystallize their options more, Germany will have been deprived of the opportunity to do better.

German policy and its economy have been troubled for some time. So it comes as little surprise that all parties promise to do better. Candidates have declared their opposition to unemployment and their support for growth. But little is said about the measures needed for change to occur.

Originally published in *The Japan Times*, September 1, 2005. Used with permission of Michael R. Czinkota and *The Japan Times*.

Taxes are talked about a lot. Discussions include the idea of confiscating income from everyone who earns more than 1 million euro, since the revenue from these 12,500 people would reduce some deficits and offend only a few voters. Other populists would supertax anyone with annual incomes above 60,000 euro. The conservatives just want to raise the consumption tax.

The lack of focus on harsh expenditure reductions (such as sharp declines in public sector salaries) indicates that in 2005 many Germans believe their tax policy to be autonomous from global competition. Also, they either forgot or never heard the Reagan message of the 1980s: "It's not the government's money, it's the taxpayer's money."

When it comes to unemployment, many intend to legislate new jobs—a tough road to competitiveness. Several facts appear to be often neglected:

- Much of the unemployment is the price of a successful, bloodless unification between East and West.
- Comparatively high levels of manufacturing employment indicate that displacements in this sector will continue to increase.
- Current problems are temporary in light of German demographic trends. Due to a severely shrinking population, soon the question will be again one of finding sufficient workers.

On occasion, the term "flexibility" is heard, but apparently immediately negated by workplace agreements that guarantee particular types of jobs for years to come. How to systematically cause the implementation of new approaches and innovative solutions is rarely mentioned. After all, tradition is highly prized here. But attention does perk up when mention is made of adjustments undergone by other economies, industries or firms—in an era of membership in the European Union, isolation from others is difficult.

Reliance on government continues to be extraordinarily high. For example, when talking about terrorism, most partners take on a don't worry attitude: The government has it all under control. As students weigh job opportunities, civil service structures still beckon very attractively—and this for graduates of business schools! No wonder that many innovative young professionals tend to leave for Britain, Norway, or Sweden.

Industry seems to be most attuned to the global realities and willing to speak out forcefully. Where politicians still vacillate about whether to get involved, say in monitoring competition from Central Europe or from China, industry is ready to talk about the pressures encountered abroad, and willing to pose tough questions to representatives of all political parties. When they hint at possible plans for the future, some exasperated entrepreneurs do not hesitate to query why action has not been taken in the past.

Individuals appear to be weary of too many campaign promises, knowing how easily they can be broken later. At the same time, close attention is paid to the actions of political leaders with the almost desperate desire to tell them and their programs apart. Even a few weeks before the election not all is said and done.

To this observer, Germany has been underperforming for many years. This election should not be decided based on glib appeals to base instincts. It is time to help voters distinguish between the short term and the long term.

Candidates need to address the meaningful issues, such as less reliance on government, trust and belief in oneself, willingness to undertake risk and obtain forgiveness for failures, and Germany's fitness in a world of economic globalization and changing regional aspirations.

A country that has come back from the devastations of World War II to furnish a pope and that maintains a position as undisputed export champion in the economic world, deserves to have a choice based on a vision, direction and confidence as was experienced last time under Chancellor Ludwig Erhard some four decades ago.

West Must be Flexible if it is Going to Assist Eastern Europe

Just when the federal government appears to be ready to take over the running of the Dude Ranch, the Eastern European members of the profession are beginning to learn about the opportunity for private sector entrepreneurship. On a recent visit through various of the newly emerging democracies, I noticed never before encountered quantities of ladies of the night in hotel lobbies, restaurants and public places. The fact that I was easily identified as a Western tourist appeared to contribute markedly

---

Originally published in *The Columbus Dispatch*, November 5, 1990. Used with permission of Michael R. Czinkota and *The Columbus Dispatch*.

to my attractiveness. The results were various conversations, a typical one of which is presented here:

O(ldest) P(rofession): You American?

R(otund) T(ourist): Yes.

OP: Interested? One thousand dollars.

RT: Isn't that a bit much? How much do you earn on your daytime job?

OP: I am a secretary and make $40 a month. Here my price is $1,000. Americans can afford it!

RT: Have you done any business yet?

OP: Not so far, but some day I will.

RT: What if I ask any of the other ladies?

OP: They also charge a thousand dollars. We are now a free market. But you have to stay with me. I talked to you first!

To assuage the sensibilities (particularly my wife's) of readers, there was no transaction. However I do believe that there was much reflection of society in these conversations.

First, the desire to become a private entrepreneur was clear. Now that restrictions are removed, the opportunity seems to beckon, and is taken advantage of. Existence of initiative, if left unchanneled, may, however, lead to unexpected and sometimes undesirable market manifestations.

Second, the idea of profit is at the forefront of the mind. However, the meaning of profit, and the understanding of the level of profitability in relationship to the existing society is totally underdeveloped. The term competition is a far cry from permeating consciousness. If we all demand the same price, then somebody has to accept! The notion of choice is not comprehended. How could it be, after—in many instances—more than half a century of suppression of individual decision-making? The value of time is different. Some day in the future seems to be a fully acceptable, if not preferable, alternative to today.

Finally, the expectations expressed and demanded bear very little relationship to reality.

The rapid conversion of the Soviet empire into a socialist league has left us breathless, but also with high hopes. The replacement of dictatorial governments, the abolishment of Communist parties, the unification of Germany and the banner-waving accompanied by shouts for democracy have lulled us into the belief that Eastern Europe has become Westernized, has become like us. Yet, the deeply ingrained differences in societal philosophies, concepts and beliefs that continue to exist are just as divisive—if not more—than political borders and may harbor the germ for continued instability and enmity.

In spite of all the smile and pledges for cooperation, we must understand that 40 years of ideology are not undone in 12 months. Rather, it will take a long time of careful transition to achieve acceptable, long-term mutual adjustment. Neglecting this need for adjustment will result in not only a political but also a human and moral failure of the Western system. What, then, are the necessary steps?

Mutual adjustment is the key. It is time to rethink perhaps some of our approaches, to move closer to out newly found partners, and to make some alterations of our own.

We need to examine the fundamental differences between societies. For example, rather than transferring our marketing expertise, accounting systems, financing schemes, production plans or management structures, we need to evaluate the degree to which their applicability must be modified in order to fit with Eastern Europe.

We must therefore reinvent our prized business fundamentals in their application to Eastern Europe. We must re-examine the role of the individual vs. the role of society in our perspective of business. We must consider the newly afforded opportunity to identify and address global problems in a global fashion. We must listen just as much as we talk. To truly help the newly emerging democracies, we have as much learning to do as they. Only we can do it easier, because of our knowledge of choice, and our sense of obligation.

Travel Advisories for the Next Generation

How does America's global role affect the lives of individuals? Currently, momentous international policy decisions are being taken; they encompass war, peace, freedom and the projection of power. It is important to step back and develop a vision of the long-term outcome of those policies for individuals. Perhaps the history of St. Paul can provide us with some direction.

Ask the State Department for travel advice, and you will be referred to the "Travel Warnings" Web site. On it, you will find many admonitions of where not to go and what not to do. For example, Syrian travel should be deferred, since protesters there have expressed anti-U.S. sentiments. Those already there should consider a speedy departure.

For Algeria, nighttime and overland travel and even a walk down the streets of Algiers are nixed. For lesser hotbeds, the standard recommendations seem to include "exercise maximum caution and take prudent

Originally published in *The Japan Times*, May 16, 2002. Used with permission of Michael R. Czinkota and *The Japan Times*.

measures. Avoid crowds, demonstrations and areas where Americans generally congregate. Keep a low profile, blend in, and don't show that you're an American!"

Left unchallenged, this advice will probably still be provided 20 years from now. It's the safe way to go, but to borrow an expression from my students, "it's so 20th century." Our policy planners need to have a vision of how our relationship with the world should be 20 years from now. Future generations should know that our policies, activities, efforts and expenditures were worth it.

A brief review of the life of St. Paul, also called the 13th apostle, may provide guidance and inspiration. Saul, as he was then known, was born about 2,000 years ago. He was a Jew and converted to Christianity. He was born in Tarsus, which made him a Roman citizen. He was an indefatigable traveler, an early globalist who wrote lots of letters.

He established churches in Asia Minor. He evangelized in Macedonia, Thessalonica, Athens, Corinth and Malta. During his life and travels, he was often met with great hostility and persecution. The Roman emperor himself was none too pleased with Paul's preaching and traveling. Christianity was not exactly popular in the reigning circles of the day.

What are the lessons here? St. Paul reached out to the world. His message was quite controversial, but it has survived quite well even until today. He was not popular for his message—but he got the word out. He was not hesitant to go to the far corners of the world of his day. In spite of all the controversy and hatred that he faced, the people he encountered abroad did not harm him. Even when he was a captive and, on orders from Rome, on his way to the eternal city, he was untouchable and treated with respect and hospitality because he was a Roman.

St. Paul's circumstances can be our guide for a vision of the future. We are proud to be Americans and the world should know it. There are special conditions associated with American citizenship—and our policies should enhance rather than hide that fact.

Some of that "specialness" is beginning to be reflected in our international policies. For example, the two captured al-Qaeda fighters who are American citizens are treated differently from the others. Despicable as their actions may have been, they are not kept in Guantanamo,

Cuba. Richard Colvin Reid is in Massachusetts, and John Walker Lindh is in Virginia. They will not face military tribunals, but rather the U.S. court process with all the legal and procedural safeguards accorded to all Americans.

This is how it should be! Another example comes from the government reaction to the kidnapping of U.S. citizens in the Philippines. In a policy reversal, the State Department has recently agreed to "make every effort" to gain the release of all Americans kidnapped overseas, even private citizens. That is good!

So where should we be in 20 years? By then, when requesting a travel advisory from the State Department, here is what I would like to hear: "As a traveler, you are advised to carry identification of being a U.S. citizen with you at all times. Wear an American flag pin to let everyone know that you are an American. This way, you will carry an umbrella of respect, safety and security. Remember, you represent your country. We wish you success in your travels."

Some might think such a vision as perhaps lacking in humility. I see it as a worthwhile goal to strive for, as a translation of national effort into individual well being, and as an outcome that will truly help bring peace to the world. After all, if Americans are secure, others will be as well.

Finding Succor in Tragedy

It is said that even the darkest cloud has a silver lining. So what positives could possibly be connected with the sorrowful destruction from Sumatra's tsunami? The catastrophe has shown us several things:

First, we all are vulnerable, be it because of our fixed location or because we go to places. In today's interlinked world, location is no longer an exposure that is the result of our birth; it is also the consequence of choice. This choice, which gives us more freedom of mobility than ever before, however, also exposes us to the consequences of our selections, which place us at the same ground zero as local populations.

Second, we are linked, even across vast distances, to outcomes both good and bad. Would popular thinking have expected natural disaster in Indonesia to also affect more than 10 other countries and visitors from dozens beyond? For many forms of danger, geographic distance is no

Originally published in *The Japan Times*, January 6, 2005. Used with permission of Michael R. Czinkota and *The Japan Times*.

longer a barrier that insulates us from the consequences of dangerous occurrences.

Third, there are important areas where we need to collaborate and where government involvement is good. In economics, the traditional textbook example has been the building of a lighthouse: Private interests might not have sufficient incentives to make the necessary investment for it, but there is a public need to make shipping safer for all.

Perhaps the example had become too dated over time; after all, who sails nowadays at night without a Global Positioning System? But the tsunami case demonstrates that the powerful forces of nature still are in charge. The example may have changed, but the need for massive international collaboration to effectively address major overarching problems has not.

Fourth, perhaps the timing and the profundity of the disaster have given us some occasion for reflection, leading to a new appreciation of the perishability of our surroundings. In the past decades we have become virtually impervious to danger—even to close personal calls. We are too much in a hurry to worry about our own lives, let alone those of others.

Here is just one example. The other day my wife opened her car door and stepped out while waving to me standing on the other side of the street. In doing so, she was nearly run over by a huge bus, which avoided her by an inch after turning very sharply.

Imagine if this had happened in days gone by in my old home in Bavaria with, say, a loose team of horses. Back then, our ancestors would surely have built a small roadside shrine devoted either to the Virgin Mary or some saint as an expression of gratitude for the miraculous rescue. For generations to come, their descendants would have gone there on the day of remembrance with renewed thanks.

What happened in our case? Well, we took a deep breath, went into a Starbucks and had a latte. Not callous, but busy! Perhaps this calamity will make us all a bit more pensive and more gratefully possessive of what we have.

The tsunami also shows us that there is a much stronger sense of world community than many have us believe. Although pundits keep predicting how we grow apart and become isolated, the outpouring of support, and aid now flowing into devastated regions is not just from governments, but from individuals who feel connected. The condolence books of embassies are filling up with comments from individuals who want to share their feelings.

It is in times like these that we are reminded why our noble forefathers founded traditional international organizations like the World Bank and the United Nations—to help, support and improve the world.

At the same time, we can see how, in an era of globalization, new icons of capitalism such as "amazon.com" and "ebay.com" are trusted and efficient collectors of funds for the needy.

President George W. Bush could round out this support by greatly downscaling the festivities planned Jan. 20 for the inauguration of his second term in office. In keeping with the themes of gratitude, humility and U.S. empathy for sudden devastation, he might suggest that the funds saved be used for the victims of the disaster, a move to be joined by political supporters and opponents alike.

It may seem unnecessary to cut back on national celebrations after the glamorous New Year festivities in Paris and Berlin, but such a step would go a long way to demonstrate that the United States intends to lead by example. What better way to demonstrate how we all are part of the world and at the same time to tangibly celebrate the beginning of a new epoch.

So yes, the disaster is tragic and will remain unforgettable. But if it wakens some new thoughts and approaches to collaboration between nations and people, then there may be a silver lining after all.

Chance to Pick Up
and Move

On May 1, the European Union will grow by 10 new members, mostly from Eastern Europe. In public, the optimism is great as is the gloating at overtaking the United States in population, gross domestic product and currency strength. In private conversations, however, there is great fear of a migration flood.

With borders opening to free passage of population, many predict disaster. Workers from low-income nations within the EU will come to

---

Originally published in *The Japan Times*, April 4, 2004. Used with permission of Michael R. Czinkota and *The Japan Times*.

steal jobs now held precariously by locals. Immigrants will take advantage of a health-care system that vastly outperforms their own at home. Then they will quickly turn out to be lazy when they see how generous the unemployment and welfare systems are structured.

And they'll never go home again once they discover the burial benefits. One can almost hear the old warning cry "close the doors, the Gypsies are coming."

The EU members-in-waiting, however, do not share such views. They point to a rich history in which they have been occupied, exploited, subjugated and oppressed. Yet, they have never left their country. Quite telling is the comment of a Hungarian who points out that "we live in brick houses"—a way of explaining that the tendency for individuals and families for centuries has been to stay in one place. Perhaps a few trips abroad, but never a move.

Reality, however, will differ from the expectations of both sides. Using the post World War II U.S. experience as a benchmark, we can develop some moving insight based on regionally consistent migration patterns.

For example, every year, on average, every seventh American moves. Most of those moves are within the same county, or within the same state. But consistently, year after year, U.S. movers to a different state approach 3 percent of the population. That is the equivalent of the entire U.S. population moving lock stock and barrel to a new home state in little over one generation.

Of course, not everybody moves. There are some groups, particularly the white, wealthy and well entrenched, who have very low permanent migration patterns—aside from certain vineyards in the summer. Those with the lowest household incomes below the poverty level are the most avid movers, seeking new economic opportunities. Also young adults move very frequently, going to college and broadening their views.

What does all this mean for the New Europe? The opportunities to pick up and move are there. The ability to prove and improve oneself as well as to achieve access to new resources are a powerful motivator for migration. Brick homes may represent culture, family and tradition, but even they are an insufficient restraint for upward mobility.

I expect the mobility of the young and not-so-well-off to increase substantially after May 1. Consider the different life expectancy levels, variations in employment rates, gaps in infant mortality rates, differences in health-care expenditures and large disparities in telephones, Internet servers or personal computers. People want to explore new options and opportunities.

The moves and behavior of the young will become an information signal for others. There emerges a tremendous opportunity to enrich the quality of life of regions as well as of individuals through these newly possible moves.

Students in European universities may well become exposed on a large scale to the famous "Hungarian mathematicians." Theater audiences may have the "Maltese Falcon" read to them by actual actors from Malta, breweries may benefit from a much greater availability of Czech brew masters.

Will all these moves leave cultures unchanged? No! Culture is the result of learned behavior and adjustment to new conditions. Opening up to others on such a gigantic scale as Europe has done within a relatively short time should bring the reward of growing flexibility, better understanding and rising tolerance levels. Mobility has brought flexibility and adjustment to the United States. It will likely change Europe forever and perhaps create a new generation of innovators and risk takers.

With relatives who live in brick houses I know the connotations of these homes in history. Perhaps now is a good time to admire the usefulness that these fixed structures once had, while moving on to the opportunities of a more flexible world.

The Falling Dollar: We'll Be on Firm Ground Again

We hear about record-breaking declines of the dollar, rising U.S. trade deficits and a retrenchment of inward investment flows. Cassandra-like voices point to the war-caused budget deficit, foresee a growing U.S. dependence on the mercy of foreigners and predict the imminent collapse of the global economy. Though these advocates of negativism are sadly mistaken, it is appropriate to review the key effects of dollar value changes together with an outlook of likely developments in 2004.

Many numbers are bandied about when it comes to the decline of the dollar. Most frequently cited is the dollar depreciation against the

Originally published in *The Washington Times*, January 5, 2004. Used with permission of Michael R. Czinkota and *The Washington Times*.

euro, with claimed declines of between 17 and 40 percent, depending on the timing of the crest and trough measurements. Here is the reality of change: When the currency under comparison is less than five years old [the euro was introduced in 1999] everything tends to be a "historic" first. The euro was introduced at an exchange rate of 1 to $1.18 and is now traded at $1.25. The historical shift in value amounts to 6 percent.

This decline has not been uniform against all currencies. It has been highly selective against the yen, the pound and the euro. Against most other currencies in Asia, Africa, or South America, there has been little change.

Theorists argue that currency shifts will alter the global flow of trade and investments. These adjustments have been very limited for several reasons: For one, between trading partners where there have not been major currency shifts, there has been no reason for adjustment, since tied currencies have kept trade and investment relations the same.

Second, many firms in the countries exposed to the currency changes have multiyear contracts and plans which take time to adjust. Many of their arrangements are with captive suppliers, meaning with plants abroad which either belong to them or contractors with long-term agreements. Therefore, even if the currency values change, suppliers do not.

Goods are often distributed by independent wholesalers, dealers, and retailers. They determine the price of any good by choosing how much of a possible price change to "pass trough" and how much to keep or absorb. Currency declines, which could be expected to lead to lower prices abroad, may mainly lead to higher profits of middlemen, while currency increases might lead to a reduction of their profits. Yet, in both cases, sales volumes might be relatively unaffected.

Most important are the decisions of customers. Buyers decide when and why they want a product, and price may only be a minor issue in making the selection. In the United States, continued strong consumer demand, which is not particularly driven by any "made in the USA" designation, accounts for strong sales of global products. In addition, significant brand preferences keep customers focused on products with only limited sensitivity to their prices. If people would really make their purchases based mainly on price, we would see a major switch of car purchases from Mercedes and Infiniti to brands made in Argentina and Malaysia, reflecting the changes in exchange rates.

So, if trade and investment flows have not changed in the past twelve months, will the big shift come now? A quake-like shift of tectonic plates is unlikely. There will be an increase in U.S. exports and a stabilization of U.S. imports. Investment decisions may be hastened or delayed. The flexibility and adjustment of economies will be important. But the values of relationships which have been built up over decades often make the cost of switching too high.

There always is a supply and demand side to all these flow equations. Central banks and other reserve institutions still prefer holding two-thirds of their currency reserves in dollars, rather than in yen or euro. The U.S. economy is growing fast. Stocks are rising rather sharply, business returns are comparatively solid—and, most importantly, the expectation and the vision are—uniquely—optimistically American.

When it comes right down to it—money is just paper. What really matters is the psychology behind it, the trust, outlook and confidence in the government which has issued the money. An old saying of traders is that "the dogs bark but the caravan keeps moving." The dollar avalanche predictors should know that there may be ups and downs, but at the end, we'll be on firm territory again.

Keys to Greater Prosperity

As we begin a new year, we look for guideposts to help governments and business improve economic performance. In a world of global competition, the platform provided to firms and individuals is crucial to growth and prosperity. From observations comparing countries that do well with those that are falling behind, here are some suggestions:

Government has few, if any, limits in coming up with new revenue-raising schemes. Such government creativity can be dangerous, become unfair and nontransparent, and go on to shape the outlook of citizens.

Let me provide one example. The state of New Hampshire recently introduced a "view factor" in its property-tax assessments. This view tax assigns a specific value to the ability to see the surrounding sights from one's property, and taxes the resulting benefit.

Originally published in *The Japan Times*, January 9, 2006. Used with permission of Michael R. Czinkota and *The Japan Times*.

In talking with audiences in a variety of countries about this new tax, there was a key difference in reactions. Some audiences were outraged about the tax, stated that the property value was already incorporated in the purchase price, and suggested that there be complaints, lawsuits or voter rebellions. Questioning the foundation and rationale of government regulations in this way seems to help the competitive platform.

On the other side, some audiences seemed more concerned with the possibility of receiving special deals under the tax: "My grandfather is blind, could he get an exemption?" "I wear glasses and can't enjoy views, could I get a reduction?" "We are only home at night, would that provide a discount?"

The latter approach reflects conditions where the basic battle has already been conceded. The argument focuses only on narrow self-interest—not helpful for a solid platform encouraging competition.

It helps to have a reluctant perspective toward taxation. The belief that any income belongs to the individual who then parts with some of it in support of government is an important constraint on government expenditures.

All too often taxation is seen as a principal government expectation with very limited regard for the person that generated the money in the first place. Such lack of concern becomes highly visible during budget discussions: Increases in expenditures are routinely seen as fixed, and any deficit is remedied through higher taxes rather than by cutting budgets.

In those rare times when a budget surplus is encountered, the tendency is to find new ways to spend money rather than return it to its proprietors. Yet, there is a remarkable lack of examples where governments have taxed their country to prosperity.

Ambition is another dimension that differs sharply and helps shape competitiveness. Of concern is not ambition per se, but the key direction of its outlook. In many countries, for example, there are regional differentials in development and economic outlook. Such inequities stir concerns and questions—which can take two entirely different directions. Letters to newspaper editors are a good indicator. They tend to describe similar situations, such as: "My former colleague has been hired by a multinational corporation and now earns four times as much as I do, even though we grew up together and have a very similar background."

It is in the concluding request and question where the writers differ. While one may ask what he or she can do to get such a good job as well, another inquires how he can bring this coworker "back to us so that we are all equal again."

The forward-driving ambition tends to work much better since it supports others and provides for more initiative and enthusiasm.

Then there is the indicator provided by conversation. When and how we talk with each other influences our perspective and horizons. Particularly when we meet new people, there is the conversational small talk that communicates little in terms of specifics, but in its cumulative thrust is reflective of society and its attitudes. Two key differences tend to emerge.

Once one gets beyond talk about the weather, key conversations in some regions will center on poor government decisions, concerns about the future of the economy, worries about factory closures, and possible future downturns in one's personal fortune. Elsewhere, one tends to find discussions focusing on new plans, ventures and opportunities that might emerge. Often the conclusion even encourages follow-up to explore mutual interests.

The upbeat conversations appear to reflect a more productive, innovative and networking society—all of which tend to be a sign of greater competitiveness.

There are other differentiators as well. The above are only some key indicators that are easy to check and seem to distinguish well among countries with different competitive platforms and reflect future economic performance. These indicators are also the ones we can influence directly and personally with our attitudes and outlooks.

So let me wish everybody: limited government creativity in raising revenue, reluctance toward budget increases, positive ambition that is supportive of others, and many forward-looking, encouraging conversations. Have a happy and prosperous New Year!

Trade Must Extend to Poorer Countries

Prosperous countries in the North, such as the United States, can no longer rely on trade between developed countries led by Fortune 500 corporations alone. Trade must increase in developing countries and transitional economies if all are to benefit from a growing world economy. Policymakers and businesses of all sizes must realize the strategic importance of the developing countries of the South, not

With D. Bélisle. Originally published in *The Japan Times*, May 31, 1999. Used with permission of Michael R. Czinkota and *The Japan Times*.

just from the traditional sociopolitical perspective, but from the perspective of fostering an integrated global economic framework. It is in everyone's best interest to respond to global trends in ways that will foster growth in all countries, including the least developed ones.

Why? Simply put, trade between firms in developing and developed countries provides the margin for expanded opportunities for trade and investment. There is a mutuality of benefit in trade, an inextricable link that contributes to economic development in all countries. Companies that export to developing countries will expand into new markets and reach consumers who are experiencing significant gains in purchasing power, and companies that import from developed countries will gain access to a supply of high-quality but cheaper products produced in conformance with international standards. This not only increases sales, but significantly improves these companies' competitive edge.

Yet the question remains: How is it possible to help developing countries while letting market forces prevail? Based on extensive research into trends in international business conducted at Georgetown's McDonough School of Business and on practical experience gained at the International Trade Center in Geneva, this article identifies those issues in international trade that will affect developing countries, outlines some initial steps taken by the ITC to help businesses and countries benefit from these global changes, and presents an opportunity not to be missed.

The three most important dimensions are trends in globalization, new forms of partnership and the rapid development of information technology.

- **Globalization.** Worldwide manufacturing and outsourcing strategies have made the production of goods cheaper, faster and better. To compete, producers must be able to measure levels of competitiveness and to correct weaknesses. Doing this requires market information, an ability to understand and forecast demand, and creativity in adapting products and finding a market niche. These requirements constitute three strikes against developing countries, who face serious limitations in undertaking the needed research and development, locating scarce trade information and utilizing more sophisticated marketing skills. Creativity and new technologies, on the other hand, present unique opportunities for the developing world to catch up with industrialized countries. Harnessing these for the benefit of developing countries is a collective challenge.

Competitiveness is the sine qua non of success anywhere. Yet to become competitive, firms in developing countries must have the capacity to measure and evaluate their overall global competitiveness. In response, the ITC has developed a "competitiveness gauge," that allows firms in developing countries to compare critical data with baseline data supplied from manufacturers around the world. Producers in any country can now compare their production, organization and other practices with those of other enterprises in the industry sector, and can therefore benchmark and improve their corporate performance.

- **Partnerships.** As developing countries foray farther into the global economy, intense teamwork between business and government and among business people themselves has become imperative. Firms and governments have to bury their mutual mistrust and foster constructive dialogue on strategies and effective collaboration. At the firm-to-firm level, businesses must begin to share costs and lessons learned. An emerging trend in the industrialized world is for companies to share the costs of infrastructure, buildings, employees, storage, transport, repairs, telecommunications systems and, in some instances, marketing costs, through dual or cross-promotion of complementary products. Developing countries have to find their own models for such joint ventures, value-added partnerships, strategic coalitions and alliances, and cooperative agreements. These are the ways of the future where risks are shared and partnerships rule the day.

The ITC has pioneered and developed a number of innovative tools and services especially for developing-country exporters using the product-network approach. It addresses key criteria for successful coopera-tion among the public and private sectors, as well as with not-for-profit organizations and agencies such as trade-promotion organizations and industry associations. Akin to Pareto's 80:20 rule, these tools are kept 80 percent the same while 20 percent are customized to respond to local needs, thus achieving economy and customization in a partnership-based approach. The Executive Forum on National Export Strategies to be held by the ITC later this year will provide a unique opportunity to review success stories of partnership-based and export-led global-development strategies.

- **Information technology.** Countries without efficient telecommunications infrastructure were long seen as doomed and excluded from such benefits of electronic commerce as faster service and shipment, more precise order transmittal, online interaction in the production process and specific forecasting of supply and demand. Yet the lack of up-to-date communication is no longer a permanent handicap. It used to be that governments regulated and controlled communication (and postal) services because only they could afford to. Today, however, the investment required to establish a basic national telecommunications system has dropped sharply, allowing private firms to bring telecommunications to any country— and to do it within two years. The question is therefore not if, but when, developing countries will participate in and benefit from trade based on global telecommunications.

As developing countries become ready to participate in the new electronic economy, the ITC serves as their one-stop shop for guidance on the implementation of overall national and business e-commerce strategies. It provides specialized training for decision-makers in firms and trade-support institutions and for government officials. It also offers advice on cybermarketing, international purchasing and the legal, finan-cial, quality and logistical aspects of e-commerce.

For both the services and product sectors, specialized services will be developed in response to needs identified through extensive research, identifying growth and use patterns and the benefits and limitations of e-commerce. In response, the ITC will provide technical assistance that focuses on e-based marketing, technological, infrastructural, strategic and legal issues. Examples are specialized programs that can match exporters and importers of fresh fruit and vegetables, profile successful service-export strategies, offer online exhibitions of products from developing countries and provide answers to the most commonly asked questions regarding e-commerce constraints.

As a result of the successful implementation of global trade agreements signed earlier this decade, international trade has reached an unprecedented volume as international growth rates in trade continue to outdistance domestic ones. Sweeping policy reforms dominated the international trade-policy debate in the early 1990s, but figuring out how to help developing countries capitalize on these staggering changes is more important today. These countries must be helped in practical ways to execute a quantum leap in terms of their economies, thus enabling them to catch up with industrialized countries.

Developing countries have to be part of the surge in global well-being, and they are ready to assume the responsibility of becoming successful partners in the global business community. As a result of profound changes under way in globalization, telecommunications infrastructure and technology, industrialized countries would be well advised to trade with firms in developing countries, not only to enhance trade and investment opportunities in this promising, prosperous world of ours, but to lower production costs, extend product life cycles, reduce costs of importing components, services and manufactured goods, and expand market access. Otherwise, chances for development, growth and stability will be jeopardized for all, North and South alike.

Bonuses and Auto Executives

Auto executives in the United States sparked a firestorm of controversy recently when they awarded huge bonuses to top industry managers. U.S. trade representative William Brock argued that any industry healthy enough to pay hundreds of millions of dollars in bonuses hardly needs continued protection from foreign competition.

The fact is that the amount paid in bonuses is minuscule in comparison to auto industry sales and profits What is bothersome about the bonuses, however, is that they symbolize the apparent willingness of U.S. auto executives to profit from the indirect tax paid by U.S. consumers through "voluntary" import restraints.

Since Japanese auto manufacturers have no incentive to export their lower-priced cars to the United States, they fill out their quota with the

Originally published in the *Chicago Tribune*, June 26, 1984. Used with permission of Michael R. Czinkota and the *Chicago Tribune*.

most expensive cars. As a result, the American consumer is forced to choose between high-priced Japanese imports and over-priced but protected U.S. cars.

One must ask, then, whether the voluntary restraints make sense. Looking back to the time of their imposition, it is clear that U.S. car manufacturers never were in danger of being noncompetitive. General Motors, for example, was not going to be driven out of the market. Without the restraints, however, the auto industry was going to face some painful readjustments, and the principle of free trade was threatened by the breadth and depth of that pain.

The United States decided at that time that the pain of readjustment was excessive [particularly in terms of the pain inflicted on elected officials] and opted to redistribute the burden among American consumers through import quotas, in the guise of voluntary export restraints.

Since the imposition of the quotas, the U.S. auto industry has staged a major comeback, and the major manufacturers reported large profits this year. Although it is good to see such improvement one must remember that much of the price for the improved profits has been paid by the American consumer.

Those who paid the price for protecting the U.S. auto industry should be rewarded by the improved industry performance. Auto executives certainly must have anticipated the public furor that arose after the announcement of the bonuses, so their decision to go ahead with the bonuses is clear proof that the U.S. auto industry has used its years of protection to become more competitive.

The only question is why the American consumer should be asked to suffer for another year.

Index

www.ingramcontent.com/pod-product-compliance
Lightning Source LLC
Chambersburg PA
CBHW062023200326
41519CB00017B/4900